Replays

of related interest

Autism, Play and Social Interaction
Lone Gammeltoft and Marianne Sollok Nordenhof
Translated by Erik van Acker
ISBN-13: 978 1 84310 520 6   ISBN-10: 1 84310 520 9

Acting Antics
A Theatrical Approach to Teaching Social Understanding
to Kids and Teens with Asperger Syndrome
Cindy B. Schneider
Foreword by Tony Attwood
ISBN-13: 978 1 84310 845 0   ISBN-10: 1 84310 845 3

The Social Play Record
A Toolkit for Assessing and Developing Social Play
from Infancy to Adolescence
Chris White
ISBN-13: 978 1 84310 400 1   ISBN-10: 1 84310 400 8

Chasing Ideas
The Fun of Freeing Your Child's Imagination
Revised Edition
Christine Durham
ISBN-13: 978 1 84310 460 5   ISBN-10: 1 84310 460 1

Giggle Time – Establishing the Social Connection
A Program to Develop the Communication Skills of
Children with Autism, Asperger Syndrome and PDD
Susan Aud Sonders
Foreword by Andrew Gunsberg
ISBN-13: 978 1 84310 716 3   ISBN-10: 1 84310 716 3

The Handbook of Gestalt Play Therapy
Practical Guidelines for Child Therapists
Rinda Blom
Foreword by Hannie Schoeman
ISBN-13: 978 1 84310 459 9   ISBN-10: 1 84310 459 8

Replays

Using Play to Enhance Emotional and Behavioral Development for Children with Autism Spectrum Disorders

Karen Levine and Naomi Chedd

Jessica Kingsley Publishers
London and Philadelphia

First published in 2007
by Jessica Kingsley Publishers
116 Pentonville Road
London N1 9JB, UK
and
400 Market Street, Suite 400
Philadelphia, PA 19106, USA

www.jkp.com

Copyright © Karen Levine and Naomi Chedd 2007
Illustrations copyright © Susan Levine 2007

Library of Congress Cataloging in Publication Data
Levine, Karen, 1959-
    Replays : using play to enhance emotional and behavioral development for children with autism spectrum disorders / Karen Levine and Naomi Chedd.
        p. cm.
    Includes bibliographical references and index.
    ISBN-13: 978-1-84310-832-0 (pbk.)
    ISBN-10: 1-84310-832-1 (pbk.)
    1. Autism in children--Treatment. 2. Autistic children--Treatment. 3. Play therapy. 4. Social interaction. I. Chedd, Naomi, 1952- II. Title.
    [DNLM: 1. Autistic Disorder--therapy. 2. Asperger Syndrome--therapy. 3. Play Therapy--methods. 4. Desensitization, Psychologic--methods. WM 203.5 L6646r 2007]
    RJ506.A9R474 2007
    618.92'85882--dc22

                                          2006029786

British Library Cataloguing in Publication Data
A CIP catalogue record for this book is available from the British Library

ISBN-13: 978 1 84310 832 0
ISBN-10: 1 84310 832 1

Printed and bound in the United States by Thomson-Shore, Inc.

To the memory of Robert H. Wharton, M.D.,
Developmental Pediatrician who could
get a giggle out of any child regardless
of illness or disability and deeply believed
in the value of doing so.

Acknowledgements

We want to thank our families, first our husbands, David Egee and Graham Chedd, who took care of "everything else" and always cheered us on as we typed and talked, talked and typed for countless hours throughout the past year. We cannot imagine completing this book without their support.

We especially want to thank the Chedd children, Harry, Kinsey, and Adam, not only for their willingness to share their mother's time, but also for serving as happy participants in Replays "beta testing," especially useful in the siblings and the technology chapters (10 and 12).

We want to thank our illustrator, Susan Levine, mother of Karen, who is in fact a "real" artist, but who was generously willing to create drawings that are not only appealing but also more closely approximate the sketches of those of us without artistic talent!

Special thanks to Maureen Branconnier who read the manuscript start to finish with two days' notice and provided invaluable input.

We are deeply appreciative of the parents who let us play with their children in what at first may seem like a strange and counterproductive way, trusting that there was method to our madness, and then joining their children in their laughter. We have learned and incorporated many variations of Replays from parents' creative individualizations over the years.

We thank the teachers who have welcomed us into their classrooms, even as we created moments of controlled chaos and from whom we have also learned many variations of Replays applications.

We also want to thank Stan Greenspan, Serena Wieder, and Barry Prizant, whose work especially inspired our own.

And, finally, a very special thank you to all the children who laugh with us and, yes, at us, as we provoke and pester them, and who fill our lives with humor, joy, and amazement as they conquer their fears and challenges with courage and gusto.

Contents

PART I

Introduction
to Replays

How this book is organized

Part I provides an overview of Replays, beginning with a sample Replay to provide a concrete example of the technique, and going on to cover background information on play therapy, an explanation of why this technique is useful and needed, and how to do Replays. Part II offers guidelines and scenarios for tailoring and adapting Replays for children with various specific developmental and social/emotional profiles. Part III offers scenarios and real-life situations, demonstrating how to tailor Replays for children working through specific sorts of challenges. Part IV guides readers in adapting Replays in a variety of settings, such as at school, in group situations, and at home with siblings, with step-by-step directions and examples. The "how to" sections (Parts III and IV) can stand alone. You don't have to read the background sections before implementing Replays. However, having some historical background and theoretical understanding will be helpful.

Sample Replay

Three-year-old Tony is non-verbal and has Pervasive Developmental Disorder (PDD). He has very little pretend play although he does like figures and dolls. He has become increasingly social over the past year and is generally a happy child, but he continues to have significant behavioral difficulties. He gets very angry very quickly, especially around transitions from favorite to less fun activities. For example, getting out of the car seat caused a major tantrum during which he was physically out of control and difficult to manage. Each time he has to have a diaper change, he has a tantrum. When he sees his mother getting a diaper out, he screams and runs the other way. As he is getting bigger and heavier, it is becoming increasingly difficult to change him. These problems occur both at home and at his preschool. The family and school use a variety of behavioral and communication supports: they use pictures to "warn" him of upcoming transitions. They use a three, two, one countdown system as any difficult transition approaches. They give him choices whenever possible, such as where he would like his diaper changed. They have also learned not to respond emotionally to his tantrums but to respond positively as soon as he calms down. These measures have all helped a bit, but the problem continues.

Tony's speech therapist began by playing with a doll with him. She had the doll pretend to drink from a toy cup. He watched with interest but didn't join in and moved away to stand closer to his mother. The speech therapist got him to give the doll a kiss, a pretend act he knew well. This was intended to get him more involved in the play. She then approached the doll with a paper towel saying "Time for your diaper change" and started to put it on the doll. The therapist made the doll begin a "tantrum," with playful sound effects and kicking. Clearly fascinated, Tony watched and smiled. He seemed to understand what she was doing and recognize it! The therapist demonstrated a few more times and Tony looked up and laughed. The therapist handed the doll to him to see if he would participate. He wasn't ready yet, and became a little anxious by this "tantrum" play. He retreated to stand next to his mother, still watching. The therapist then had the doll "settle down" and allow itself to be changed and be happy. The therapist suggested to the parents to do this sort of play several times a day around issues that were difficult for Tony, including other transitions such as getting out of the car and getting ready for bed. Soon he began also to participate in the demonstrations. He was then ready for short Replay picture stories. As he was young and non-verbal, it was important to keep the stories very short and have only three or four pictures. While this alone did not fix all the transition problems right away, diaper changes began to be easier, and Tony and his parents now had a way to "talk about" his feelings about these events. Often beginning the Replay before the actual diaper change or transition to the car seat helped Tony express his feelings through play and gradually eliminated many of his actual behavioral upsets.

1

Introduction

If it's not fun, why do it?

— Jerry Greenfield of Ben & Jerry's

Replays is a fun, easy-to-learn, play-based approach developed to help children who have behavioral difficulties due to intense responding. While this specific technique is new, it is couched in a very long history of using play as a therapeutic medium for working with children who are having difficulty coping with challenging emotions.

What are the mechanisms by which Replays works?

Children who have rapid, intense and often negative emotional and behavioral reactions to seemingly small events (e.g. haircuts; broken toys; loud noises; changes in schedules; taking medicine) literally "practice" with adult support, by re-experiencing these events in the context of playful, exaggerated, and symbolic re-enactment. Often children want to play the event over and over again as they "master" it. The child takes on different roles (e.g. himself as the star in the event; the person causing the problem by pretending to be the barber). The adult adds humor to help relax the child and make the re-experiencing pleasurable and creative. When the event occurs the next time, the child has had so much practice that the previously learned emotional reaction of extreme upset often greatly diminishes. In some cases, the upsetting situation is "fixed" immediately; in others, reactions diminish over time and with repeated re-enactments.

Who can benefit from Replays?

Replays can help children with a variety of developmental disabilities who have difficulties regulating strong emotions. Children across the PDD spectrum, including Asperger's syndrome, Pervasive Developmental Disorder – Not Otherwise Specified (PDD–NOS) and autism, and children with other developmental disabilities, who have challenges with emotional and behavioral regulation, have reacted positively to this intervention. Because Replays relies on use of some symbolic skills, a symbolic play and communication level of at least about 18 months is usually a prerequisite for this technique to be effective. However, some children have responded positively although they have not yet shown symbolic play skills. This is due to the high emotional quality and familiarity of the schema, making this format readily accessible on some level.

Who should do Replays with a child?

This technique can be implemented by parents, teachers, therapists, and other caregivers. It is relatively easy to learn and fun to do. However, the adult needs to know the child well enough to understand what types of situations are difficult, some details about that situation, and to have ongoing opportunities to play in an engaging way with the child. With practice and willingness to experiment, Replays is an enjoyable and therapeutic intervention that can be implemented in a variety of settings by virtually any professional or caregiver who works with children with regulatory problems.

To provide the context of this technique, we begin with a brief overview of the history of play therapy – where and when it originated, and how it has been used over the past century. A multi-faceted intervention, play therapy has its roots in the work of some of psychology's greatest thinkers and theorists, beginning with Sigmund Freud. It is largely a twentieth-century phenomenon, like the field of psychology itself.

Before the turn of the twentieth century, play was considered by most philosophers and chroniclers of human behavior not as a process critical to healthy human development, but rather as a way of getting rid of excess energy (Von Schiller 1794). Certainly it wasn't considered therapeutic. It was not until Sigmund Freud postulated that play was, in part, a child's actively repeating a traumatic event that was experienced passively in order to gain some control over it that it garnered more interest and acceptance. Sigmund Freud first used play therapy with children – his colleague's child – in the early years of the twentieth century (Freud 1909).

Since then, much has been written on the subject. Anna Freud, daughter of Sigmund Freud, and Austrian psychoanalyst Melanie Klein are among the first names to be associated with the use of play as a therapeutic intervention (see *Play Timeline* by James Drisko, Smith College School for Social Work, expanded from *The History of Play Therapy* by D. L. Rheaumes, downloaded from the internet, July 2000). Carl Rogers' person-centered approach led to a greater emphasis on the relationship between therapist and client. But it was Virginia Axline whose work in the late 1940s (Axeline 1947), gave rise to the more recent variations of play-based approaches by incorporating the idea that children can, through play, resolve their own problems. This forms the basis of many interventions in the field today.

There have been several substantial movements and program models for intervention with children, incorporating many principles of play and play therapy to work with children with autism. Greenspan, Wieder and Simons (1998) have developed a comprehensive approach to fostering development in children with autism and other developmental disabilities, through play, using techniques of their Floor Time/Developmental Individual Differences model. Susan Aud Sonders developed an easily accessible "how to" approach in *Giggle Time* (2003), building also on the work of Barry Prizant and Stanley Greenspan for using high-affect, playful social routines to establish the beginnings of interaction and communication. *Relationship Development*

Intervention (Gutstein and Sheely 2002) is an adult-led, play-based model teaching increasingly complex reciprocal interaction focusing on non-verbal pragmatic development. These models all offer exciting techniques, capitalizing on the adults' capacity to engage the child's emotional system through high-motivation interactive experiences, and then building increasing social complexity into these interactions. Replays is fully compatible with these techniques, based in the same set of principles, but addressing a very specific aspect of development – emotional regulation – using a specific set of strategies.

Replays draws from these and several other schools of play therapy. Although each approach differs slightly, all are in agreement on several points:

1. The relationship between the adult and child is critical. There must be trust or the likelihood that it can develop.

2. The adult must be authentic and committed to exploring the child's world through play with the child.

3. The goal is to help the child grow in some way: such goals may include developing a better understanding of a behavior, changing a behavior, feeling less anxiety or anger about specific events or routines, feeling more in control of a frightening situation, or participating in and/or enjoying a particular activity that has been inaccessible previously.

Replays also draws on the principles involved in "systematic desensitization," a behavioral technique initially developed by Joseph Wolpe (1996), for treating adults with specific phobias such as fear of snakes. In this technique, the adult is taught relaxation strategies and to think of happy things, while learning to tolerate increasing exposure to the feared object. In Replays, the adult engages the child in gradually increasingly realistic play representing an upsetting event. The re-enactment of this event is accompanied by happy emotions in the child, rather than the upset emotions the child previously has associated with the event. These happy emotions are generated through the adult's techniques of exaggeration and a generally playful approach, combined with the inherent reassuring safety of the medium of pretend play.

This integration of the child play-centered philosophy of play therapy with the highly structured adult-led technique of systematic desensitization may seem somewhat contradictory. For typically developing children dealing with emotional challenges, the child generally takes the lead within the play therapy, and the adult supports the child's play. The child's play evolves without overt adult structuring, so that the adult and child together meander down a path through which they explore and resolve what is upsetting to the child. Systematic desensitization, in contrast, is essentially a "therapist-led" highly structured approach. Because children on the autism spectrum do not typically engage naturally in much pretend play, let alone use it to help them naturally resolve emotional problems, in using play for this purpose in this population, the adult takes the lead and "teaches" the techniques of symbolic play, in the process of the play. The adult leads the child in content and technique, in order for the child to learn to use play in this way. However, while the adult leads, the adult's choice of content of the play, including the played-through emotional responding, is fully individually tailored, derived from the child's own experiential repertoire, just as the natural play of typically developing children is. Hence, the child's experiences and responses form the basis of the content of Replays.

Further, the child controls the specifics of the steps of the play, including the complexity of the symbolic component, the "proximity" to reality, and the style of humor that effectively generates happy feelings in the child, based on the child's emotional responses, which guide the adult. For example, if a child is enjoying the play and taking an increasingly active role, the chances are that the adult has found just the right balance of realism and playfulness. If the child is fearful, the adult has started "too close to home." If the child enjoys it but does not begin to participate, the adult is likely creating too complex or lengthy a scenario for the child's level of pretend.

While play therapy and systematic desensitization are well-established techniques, they are not generally used in combination, and not with children on the autism spectrum, a group for whom pretend play of this sort is not a naturally developing skill. Hence, Replays combines somewhat disparate approaches and applies these to a population who can, through this approach, both develop symbolic skills, and work, through play, to master upsetting emotions.

Finally, Replays also builds on the principles of cognitive behavioral therapy, (CBT) (e.g. Beck 1979; Graham 1998), a treatment approach typically used for highly verbal and typically developing older children and adults. This is currently a primary recommended and often remarkably effective treatment for older children and adults with "mood disorders," which are states of intense maladaptive emotional responding and hence related to the emotional regulation issues treated by Replays. CBT involves verbally educating the client regarding their cognitive distortions of their experiences that are causing their intense emotional responding, and then teaching them new ways to interpret experiences as well as relaxation and other techniques to decrease the intensity of emotional responding. This technique relies heavily on the ability to talk about one's interpretation of upsetting situations, as well as one's emotional experiences and responses. For a young child on the autism spectrum, it would be as gratifying as it would be ludicrous to be able to achieve emotional and behavioral change through this sort of language-based metacognitive process (e.g. "You go into a rage when I bring out the toothbrush because you think it will cause you agonizing pain, but if you can think of it as helping your teeth to stay healthy, and relax while I do it, you won't mind it.").

Tony Attwood, renowned Asperger specialist, has written a very helpful initial guide to adapting this technique for adolescents with Asperger's, compensating for difficulties understanding, and discussing emotional experiences and response by incorporating use of visuals, emotional "thermometers," co-observing and discussion of videotaped experiences, and actual teaching and practice of what is entailed in expressing and interpreting emotions (Attwood 2003). Replays incorporate some of these adaptations but puts them into more immediate experiential and minimally verbal form for the younger and less verbal population targeted.

There have also been efforts to adapt CBT to young children through adult-guided play therapy (e.g. Knell 1993). In this approach, as in Replays, the adult uses props, and guides the play to help the child learn new coping strategies to upsetting experiences. This approach adapts adult-based cognitive behavioral therapy for use with typically developing preschoolers and young children experiencing emotional problems.

We also combine play and adult-led problem solving, further adapting it to be useful not only for young children, but for children on the autism spectrum, who don't naturally use pretend and have little to no capacity to "talk about" their emotions, or perhaps talk at all. Through Replays, the "language" is that of emotions and play, both the familiar emotional sequence the child experiences, as well as happy playful emotions the child is also able to experience. Through this shared non-verbal or minimally verbal "language," the adult helps the child to experience and re-experience, and in this way "talk about" his intense emotional reactions and experiences and at the same time learn new, more adaptive responses. Hence Replays can be considered as "affective behavioral play-based intervention," working directly through the child's affective system, using play, to impact his behavior.

If you work with children, as your patients, your students, or your own, you may already incorporate some of these techniques into your own practice. How can Replays further enhance your work?

Replays is a technique developed to help children who have significant regulatory difficulties learn to cope with their own strong emotions. Replays, in the context of play, helps children to re-experience events that are upsetting to them, thereby helping to increase their capacity to control their own strong emotions and subsequent behaviors. The technique combines the use of pretend play and strong emotions as in Floor Time (Greenspan, Wieder and Simons 1998), and picture-based stories similar to those in Social Stories™ (Gray and White 2002). Replays, however, focuses directly on the child's individual and intense emotional experiences. Replays can be used in conjunction with other tools and interventions, such as behavioral management techniques, sensory integration, Floor Time, Social Stories™, environmental adaptation, and, in some instances, psychotropic medication.

We hope you are able to positively impact the children you are working with by adding your own personal touches to your Replays. Above all else, have fun!

References

Attwood, T. (2003) Cognitive Behaviour Therapy. In L. Holliday Willey (ed.) *Asperger Syndrome in Adolescence: Living with the Ups, the Downs and things in Between*. London: Jessica Kingsley Publishers.

Axeline, V.M. (1947, 1969) *Play Therapy*. New York: Ballantine Books.

Beck, A. (1979) *Cognitive Therapy and the Emotional Disorders*. New York: Penguin Books.

Drisko, J.W. A Short History of Play Therapy. Avaliable at http://sophia.smith.edu/~jdrisko/playtimeline.htm Accessed July 2000.

Freud, S. (1909) Analysis of a Phobia in a Five-year-old Boy. In *The Standard Edition of The Complete Works of Sigmund Freud: Two Case Histories "Little Hans" and "The Rat Man"*. Vol.10, 2004. New York: Vintage.

Greenspan, S.I., Wieder, S. and Simons, R. (1998) *The Child with Special Needs: Encouraging Intellectual and Emotional Growth*. Reading, MA: Perseus Books.

Graham, P. (1998) *Cognitive Behavior Therapy for Children and Families*. Cambridge: Cambridge University Press.

Gray, C. and White, A.L. (2002) *My Social Stories Book*. London: Jessica Kingsley Publishers.

Gutstein, S.G. and Sheely, R.K. (2002) *Relationship Development Intervention with Children, Adolescents and Adults: Social and Emotional Development Activities for Asperger Syndrome, Autism, PDD and NLD*. London: Jessica Kingsley Publishers.

Knell, S. (1993) *Cognitive-Behavioral Play Therapy*. Lanham, MD: Jason Aronson Publishers.

Sonders, S.A. (2003) *Giggle Time – Establishing the Social Connection: A Program to Develop the Communication Skills of Children with Autism, Asperger Syndrome and PDD*. London: Jessica Kingsley Publishers.

Von Schiller, J.C.F. (1794) Letters Upon the Aesthetic Education of Man. In (c.1910) *Literary and Philosophical Essays: French, German and Italian. With Introduction and Notes*. New York: Collier Series: The Harvard Classics, 32.

Wolpe, J. (1996) *The Practice of Behavior Therapy*. Tarrytown, NY: Pergamon Press.

2

Understanding Children's Intense Responding and how Replays Helps

You can discover more about a person in an hour of play than in
a year of conversation.

— Plato

What is the process that causes some children to have extreme reactions
to seemingly small events?

Children who have difficulty managing and regulating their
emotions tend to reach uncomfortable heights of anger or distress. They
may reach these peaks more frequently, more rapidly and more
intensely than other children. Seemingly small events that may mildly
or briefly upset another child can cause a child with these difficulties to
become severely agitated or upset. A broken or lost toy, an unexpected
schedule change, the end of a favorite activity, a loud noise or a change
in the environment may cause intense agitation. This agitation may
begin without warning and rapidly escalate – that is, the child may seem
fine one minute and devastated moments later. Further, the degree of
upset may be much greater than the situation seems to warrant, and the
child may have difficulty calming.

Once the child is upset, efforts to calm or console him with soothing
talk or a hug, or implementing behavior management techniques such

as "time outs," typically fail. Once the child has regrouped, the incident is over and activities move on. Hence, the child experiences a sequence of happy play, then explosion, then calming and resuming activity. While this sounds reasonable and desirable, the child may not have a clear understanding of the details of the "explosion." He may not fully remember the sequence of events or even the event that led up to the emotional upset. The next time a similar event occurs he is likely to have a similar response. His emotions escalate so rapidly that he does not have an opportunity to learn from his experience and form a new way of responding. He has no time or mechanism by which to generate an understanding of the situation or a new response pattern.

Learned emotional avoidance

Additionally, many children who have difficulty coping with their own intense emotions may also have difficulty coping with the intense emotions of others. They may become frightened or upset if someone is sad, angry or crying. They may avoid such scenes in books or videos. These children may actually develop a fear of emotions in general. Some children can become emotionally "shut down" or even depressed as they attempt to avoid experiencing what might seem to be an out-of-control or agitated state. Some children reach a point at which they cannot tolerate hearing words such as "mad" or "sad." These children have essentially learned to avoid or suppress emotions, because they are dangerous in that they can result in an unmanageable state, just as someone who is allergic to peanuts learns to avoid them.

Problems occur on two levels with this pattern of intense responding. The first level is the children's emotional response. They respond too intensely for their own comfort. They quickly escalate to an intolerable state, one far beyond reason. This is unpleasant for the child and clearly for those around the child. In this state, they cannot modulate their behavior, nor are they open to reason or learning coping skills. This results in the second level: the behavior the child engages in when they are in this state, including screaming and crying, full-blown tantrums or even aggression.

This pattern of responding is adaptive, as the child's strong behavioral response generally causes the unpleasant situation to change in some way. For a dysregulated infant, for example, who is bothered by every mildly unpleasant sensation and with little capacity to self-calm, the pattern of reaching a howling state as quickly as possible is adaptive. It usually brings an adult to the rescue. This "emergency calling system" is an excellent survival mechanism. However, as children mature, their nervous system increasingly develops the capacity to tolerate mildly unpleasant sensations. Further, they acquire more specific and effective means to impact their environment, such as non-verbal and verbal communication. At this point the "instant emergency state" is no longer the child's most effective means of altering his environment in the desired way. In fact, it becomes primarily maladaptive; when the child reaches an unpleasant state, he is unable to continue in what might overall be a pleasant activity. He may become too agitated to communicate with those around them who could potentially fix their source of agitation. Further, the child typically receives negative feedback from others in response to an outburst.

Emotional adaptation

Why would a child repeatedly engage in a maladaptive pattern of responding? There are essentially two reasons:

1. It is human nature to continue to do what was once adaptive and functional, even when it is no longer so. Charles Darwin, one of the earliest scholars of human behavior, writes about this phenomenon in *The Expression of the Emotions in Man and Animals* (1872):

    >...movements which are serviceable in gratifying some desire, or in relieving some sensation, if often repeated, become so habitual that they are performed, whether or not of any service, whenever the same desire or sensation is felt, even in a very weak degree. (p.345)

    In other words, an emotional response, which may once have been adaptive and occurs many times in response to a specific type of situation, can eventually become a habit, even though it is no longer adaptive. Many children with this pattern of extreme responding were quite dysregulated as infants, crying easily with difficulty self-calming. In infancy, this pattern caused the caregiver to continually attend to their discomforts and provide external calming. As they grow older, many children develop increased physiological capacity to calm themselves, yet continue in their old "habitual" patterns, having had no opportunity to develop new emotional responding patterns.

2.   Given that the natural tendency is to continue responding in the same way, what process occurs in typically developing children to cause change in emotional response that is not occurring in children with this more intense and rapidly escalating style of response? Why does any emotional response change over time? Typically developing children whose emotional responding is less intense and more differentiated have many opportunities to experiment with more adaptive responses. When a toy breaks, a typical toddler may whimper, hand it to an adult who fixes it and then return to being happy. The next time a toy breaks, he may not even whimper, but just feel a little frustrated and then hand it to the adult to fix, remembering that last time this was how he became happy again. The child who responds to the broken toy by flying into an uncontrollable rage, or has a complete and long-lasting emotional breakdown, doesn't have an opportunity to experience a small amount of upset and work out a solution. Hence, this particular responding pattern, with its speed and intensity, precludes opportunities for learning a more adaptive pattern. The child cannot learn from experience that a small amount of upset and a request for help would bring on calm happiness more effectively than an emotional explosion. In fact, the child does not emotionally "know" that a small amount of upset is possible, having not experienced it.

Unlearning emotional responses

In order to learn emotional regulation, one must be able to experience small amounts of emotion and develop a calm way of acting and responding to this emotion that offers relief. A child must learn, through experience, to have a less intense emotional response, and then be able to problem solve regarding how to "fix" this unpleasantness. Barkley (1997), discussing the steps involved in emotional regulation, writes that

> The capacity to interrupt an ongoing sequence of behavior is likewise critical to self-regulation…the behavioral inhibition component must nevertheless become engaged to halt the current stream of responses in order to permit such analysis, synthesis and midcourse correction to occur and to thereby redirect the motor programming and execution system to this new tack of responding. (p.161)

A child who responds quickly and intensely does not get the opportunity to develop new patterns of responding. As every caregiver knows, trying to reason with or teach a child in the midst of a tantrum, even a highly verbal and typically developing child, is a fruitless endeavor! Further, explaining to a child with this intense emotional responding pattern, especially a child who has other developmental or communication difficulties, is not effective.

How, then, can a child with this responding pattern be taught new patterns? In order to help the child learn, it is necessary to slow down and dilute the intensity of the experience for the child. Helping the child to re-experience the event through play and story enables them to slow down the experience, learn the sequence of events and practice responding, thus preparing him to inhibit his own behavior in the heat of the moment. While the child cannot slow down their own experiences and change course in the middle of severe distress, the adult can assist the child in re-experiencing the event at a slow pace and with a small and manageable amount of emotion, thereby facilitating the development of new response sequences. This process of assisting the child to re-experience the event in a safe environment, in which the child is able to stay relatively calm, is the purpose of Replays.

How does Replays help the child?

Replays is a technique that actually teaches new emotional and behavioral responding patterns in the same situations that have brought on old and maladaptive responses. Through practice, in play, and then in a story, the child repeatedly re-experiences the type of incident that usually brings on a strong response, yet elicits a lesser emotional response when it is removed from the actual experience. In this way, the child develops increased understanding of and control over his or her emotions. After an upset has occurred and the child has recovered, the adult (parent, therapist or teacher) re-enacts the event with the child, especially the child's emotions, and subsequent recovery. They act it out several times. The adult may first have to do all of the acting out. The child will likely watch, perhaps at first in an anxious state, then (almost always) quite interested.

There are many other approaches that are used for such challenges, including positive behavior management, sensory integration, Social Stories™ and psychotropic medication. Each of these interventions attacks the problem from a different angle. Each can be beneficial, and several techniques can be used in combination. Replays can be used in conjunction with any of these techniques.

Replays combines aspects of several different intervention approaches. As in traditional child play therapy, play is used as a tool to work through and help the child master what he or she has experienced as traumatic. Like Floor Time, a variation of traditional play therapy (Greenspan, Wieder and Simons 1998), Replays uses the natural emotions of the child as a way to reach the child. Additionally, in both Replays and Floor Time, the adult uses his or her own genuine emotions to activate the emotional system of the child as a basis for learning. But, unlike the Floor Time model or traditional child play therapy, Replays is quite adult-structured, with the adult directing the topic and sequence of the play, at least initially.

Replays also employs the technique from Social Stories™ (Gray 1995), that of using a story with pictures, usually photographs to begin with, from the child's life to help the child understand sequences of events and behaviors. Unlike Social Stories™, however, the story in

Replays focuses on the child's own emotional response and subsequent emotional recovery, helping the child re-experience and adapt his or her own emotional process. Whereas the goals of Social Stories™ are to help the child understand others' social cues and learn appropriate behaviors, the primary goal of Replays is to help the child re-experience and increasingly emotionally tolerate troubling situations, thereby learning new emotional sequences of responding.

Replays also incorporates the behavioral concept of "systematic desensitization," which is often used to help overcome phobias, such as fear of snakes. The fearful person gets comfortable at a far distance from a caged snake while engaged in a relaxing activity, and then gradually gets closer while relaxing, until they are happily letting the snake crawl on them. Small amounts of fear are paired with relaxation and pleasant sensations; exposure to the feared stimulus gradually increases; and tolerance gradually increases. Similarly, in Replays, the child experiences small amounts of emotional distress in the safe context of play, far from the intensity of the actual situation, and with a trusted adult. Re-experiencing the distress in small and manageable amounts associated with positive emotions allows the child to form a new emotional sequence. Whereas previously the child was used to the pattern of "upsetting event → extreme distress," now the child can experience repeatedly, in play and in looking through the story, the sequence of the upsetting event, followed by a small amount of emotional upset, and ultimately calming.

Replays attacks the problem directly at the level of the child's emotions. Replaying helps the child develop a sense of mastery over a situation that was previously extremely upsetting. This mastery is both cognitive and emotional. In sports, athletes use "instant replays" on video to slow down and hence understand events that happen very quickly in the heat of the moment. Similarly, with Replays, the event slows down, and the child is able to develop a detailed cognitive understanding of what led up to the upset as well as what calmed him or her again. Emotionally, the child experiences small and manageable amounts of the upset but remains in control.

Success through repetition

Further, by creating new solutions at the end of the Replay, the child can practice a more adaptive alternative to becoming upset. Through replaying the event several times, he or she can experience the initial emotions but with less intensity each time. By helping the child experience this with a trusted adult, in a playful fashion, and "hamming it up" together, the child can experience the triggers to extreme upset, but at the same time actually feel calm and happy feelings. He or she learns a new sequence: "troubling event → small amount of upset feeling → recovery."

As previously mentioned, the first few times an adult facilitates play through the event, the child may be a little anxious, although very interested, much like an adult watching a scary movie. After playing through it several times and having a story of the event, however, usually children want to play through the "climax" of the story over and over, and often seek out the story, studying the pictures with great interest, especially of the upsetting emotions, but without experiencing distress. The child often becomes a student of his or her own emotional response.

Who can Replays help?

Children with regulatory difficulties characteristic of a variety of developmental disabilities can benefit from Replays. This includes many children with Asperger's syndrome, PDD–NOS, autism, Williams syndrome, and Prader-Willi syndrome. In general, a symbolic or communication level of at least 15–18 months is needed. However, Replays can sometimes be successful with children who do not yet have sophisticated pretend play skills. Replays may also be successful with children who have little or no verbal language. It works because the story and feelings portrayed are so familiar and of major significance to the child. Some children who do not engage spontaneously in pretend play, such as feeding a doll or putting a figure in a car, will understand Replays on some level and will join in. Replays may even provide a way to begin to teach pretend play. Of course there are some children who will not have the symbolic capacity to respond to this technique. For these children, the many other techniques mentioned earlier can be helpful, and it may be that at a later point in development Replays will become more accessible.

Is there a down side?

Sometimes parents or teachers are hesitant to try this technique, because they are concerned that focusing on the unpleasant event or the undesirable behavior might encourage the child to repeat undesirable behavior or cause more upset. In fact, it is usually the opposite. In traditional play therapy, the therapist helps the child play through and re-experience their traumas to gain control over them. Children with PDD or anxiety disorders, too, seem to gain relief through the play itself, and increasingly gain control over their emotions and feelings. Clearly, positive behavioral management techniques (e.g. rewarding for desired behavior) or more aggressive behavioral management programs (e.g. time out for hair-pulling) should also continue as the first response to undesired or unsafe behavior. However, replaying the event later, rather than "in the moment" will reinforce alternative and more appropriate behaviors.

References

Barkley, R.A. (1997) *ADHD and the Nature of Self-control*. New York: The Guilford Press.

Darwin, C. (1872) General Principles of Expression. In P. Ekman (ed.) (1998) *The Expression of the Emotions in Man and Animals*. New York: Oxford University Press.

Gray, C.A. (1995) Teaching Children with Autism to "Read" Social Situations. In K. Quill (ed.) *Teaching Children with Autism*. New York: Delmar Publishers Inc.

Greenspan, S.I., Wieder, S. and Simons, R. (1998) *The Child with Special Needs: Encouraging Intelectual and Emotional Growth*. Reading, MA: Addison-Wesley.

3

How to do Replays

Man is a make believe animal. He is never so truly himself than when he is acting a part.

— William Hazlitt

1. Pick an event
    Pick an event that is predictably troublesome for your child and happens fairly frequently. It may be a specific, regularly occurring event such as getting in the car seat, staying seated at mealtimes or going to bed at night. It could be more general, such as when a toy breaks or a puzzle piece or favorite video cannot be found. It could be a fear or anxiety reaction, such as fear of a particularly loud voice, dogs, or going to the doctor. Or it could be a sensory challenge such as getting unexpectedly splashed, wet or dirty, hearing a loud noise (thunder), or getting a haircut. It's important to choose an event that happened recently, was upsetting to the child and is likely to happen again, so it will be fresh and active in the child's emotional world.

2. Re-enact the event
    Soon after the upset has occurred, but not when the child is still very upset, re-enact the event using props that will make it meaningful to the child. If the child is only just beginning to pretend and has little language, you may need to play through the event at the actual place where it happened. For example, consider a three-year-old child with PDD who is continually standing up in his high chair, is continually told to sit down

but gets up again and again, sometimes even catching a parent's eye and being purposely mischievous. The adult can put a favorite toy, such as a Winnie-the-Pooh doll in the high chair with the child, have it stand up, say "No! Sit DOWN!" and have the doll sit down. The child may only watch fleetingly. A few more demonstrations, perhaps adding Pooh starting to stand up, then the adult pretending to angrily catch him may capture the child's interest and help him make the connection between his behavior and Pooh's. With repetition and playful, exaggerated affect, he will begin to see the cause and effect: Pooh stands up → parent scolds him. So, if the child stands up, the parent may scold him too.

For a child who is more advanced in pretend and symbolic play, the Replay need not be immediately tied to the actual event and can be more abstract. If a child is a fussy eater, for example, and habitually spits out or throws food, the adult can incorporate exaggerated spitting or throwing food into a play scenario involving dolls in a dollhouse at a later time. This almost always gets a reaction of amusement from even the youngest children; they can't resist the dramatic sound affects and "inappropriate" behavior by adults! Then the adult can demonstrate more acceptable behavior and language: "I want to spit my peas out...but I won't. I'll just eat one and just push the rest over to one side." With playful repetition in a variety of settings (home, at day care or school or at Grandma's house), they usually recognize it as their own behavior.

The first few times you may have to go through the event in a short and quick version, to "hook" the child. Be sure to make the emotional components, e.g. the events immediately preceding and following the upset, really interesting and very emotional. Once the child seems to understand the pretend game, try to get him or her to participate at whatever level is possible. Slow down the event and see if you can get the child to tell you or show you what to do by pausing, or handing him or her the doll. For example, make the Pooh doll sit down and say "I'll be good...no, I'm going to STAND..." and see if the child can say "...UP!", or can make the doll stand up. Begin to say "NO!" and see if the child can take on that role. You may have to playfully coach the child through it, but as long as the play holds his or her interest, you have found a good pace and level. Use "theatrical license" and ham it up to keep the child interested. Exaggeration both makes the play interesting and also allows the child to experience the happy desirable feeling of playful humor combined with a stressful event.

3.   Make a story of the event

Once the child has demonstrated a good understanding of the play, the adult can create a Replay story. This does not need to be immediate, but should be available within the next day or so such that the event and the play are still fresh in the child's mind. Some children benefit from this visual "post Replay" story while for others it is unnecessary or not of interest. It is generally worth trying because, when children like it, it gives the Replay more power through increased opportunity for review.

The Replay story, like a Social Story™, is a series of captioned pictures. It should be very short, three to four pages, for younger or less advanced children, and can be longer for children whose play is more sophisticated and complex. For some children, each component can be more than one page, allowing you to add interesting details and hold the child's attention. The story should include, at least, the following:

i.   a happy picture (the child is sitting in his or her high chair eating), then,

ii.   an event (the child standing up in his or her high chair, grinning), then, either as part of the same page or the next page,

iii. an upset picture (Mommy saying "NO" with an angry face and the child crying), then

iv.   a happy resolution (the child sitting down eating and Mommy smiling).

While the adult should not worry *at all* about artistic merit, the facial expressions should be clear and easy to interpret. Details such as an open mouth, hand held up, pointing, and knit brow for angry yelling, tears for sadness and so forth can get the emotions across. Since children on the autistic spectrum often miss or misinterpret facial expressions and non-verbal cues, this offers an additional teaching opportunity. For example, all sad faces can be red and all happy and comforting faces can be blue, while angry faces are always green. Experimenting with color and size of details that the child notices, such as logos on toys, eye-glasses, or correct hair style and color will help him or her identify people and interpret actions. Actual photographs can also be used but usually are not necessary. If the child has sufficient abstraction skills to respond to the pretending, he or she will also be able to respond to the sketched story. Images downloaded from the internet or other visual picture programs can also be used. It helps to include written captions, even for non-verbal children, so the story can be told to the child in the same way each time, and by more than one adult or an older peer.

One picture per page is recommended, so the child can process each component separately, and sequencing doesn't become an issue. However, some children can follow more than one picture on a page.

Troubleshooting tips
What if the child gets upset when you start to play?

Some children may become anxious when the adult begins to replay an upsetting event. The anxiety may stem from associating the event, or any mention of it, with being "in trouble." One child who was replaying a sequence involving pulling his sister's hair immediately leapt into the therapist's lap, yelling "No 'time out'!" The anxiety can also stem from the reminder of an intense feeling. A very strong initial reaction does suggest that this is an important area and the child needs help in working through it.

In either case, the adult can simply create more distance between the play and the actual event by using several strategies:

1.   The adult can use animals (soft toys, favorite movie or TV character) rather than people dolls.

2.   The adult can slightly alter the events, e.g. instead of having one doll pull another doll's hair, have one doll hit another or take the other doll's toy, or have one tiger pull another tiger's tail.

3.   The adult can make the play very short, e.g. one very quick pull then a hug and be friends again, then a quick pull, then a hug.

Once the child understands that it is just fun play, with no real consequences, he or she will very likely want to join in. A little anxiety at first can hold the child's interest and often indicates that you are touching on an important event or issue.

What if the child takes the play in a different direction?

Keep trying! The first few times you may want to follow the child's lead, as it may be a related story. As long as the child incorporates a similar sort of upset, it may be productive. However, sometimes more advanced children will take the play in a different direction to avoid thinking about a difficult situation or experiencing an upset. You can, in very small doses, continue to re-introduce the upsetting event through the story. You may want to take on the upsetting role and very quickly "feel all better." You don't want to actually upset the child, but you want to get close enough to the troubling issue so that the child can re-experience and begin to master it. This is much like trying to engage an adult in a discussion about an upsetting event in order to resolve it, but he keeps changing the subject!

Sometimes children don't understand what you are trying to get them to play. You can be more aggressive, directive or dramatic than you might ordinarily be. Yell louder, use exaggerated facial expression or movement, or add sound effects. It may take several "instant replays" of the event before the child understands, especially if you are playing in an uncharacteristic way.

What if the child does not seem interested or doesn't catch on?

Not all children can engage in or benefit from Replays. However, if the child has some pretend skills, he probably will be able to access Replays on some level. Some tips for gaining the child's attention include the following:

- Keep the replay of the story short. Most events can be abbreviated to two or three lines of dialogue. This may keep the attention of a child who is not able to sustain interest or who is a little bit alarmed.

- If the child simply does not seem to understand, exaggerate the emotion and make it sillier or more playful. Use high-pitched, pretend crying or have a pretend tantrum with real kicking. Children enjoy watching adults act silly!

- If the child is upset, use a more abstract or slightly different version of the event or reduce the display of emotion. You may also include a favorite toy, event or occurrence, such as using two trains that have a race or get into an argument, or two dolls who get caught in a rainstorm.

What if the child wants to play the event over and over?

Some children want to replay the event a seemingly endless number of times. Once a child has mastered the story, use it to create variations and continue to increase tolerance for related emotions and events. As long as the child finds it interesting to play, it is probably helping him come to terms with mastering the emotion. Of course the adult may grow tired of it and then it is fine to stop! The child can continue to play by using the picture story in other settings, alone or with another adult, sibling or peer.

What if you can't draw?

Even limited artistic skills are good enough for this purpose. One mother successfully used picture communication symbols to represent the emotions and events. Her son was already familiar with the symbols and could easily learn to "read" his stories on his own. You can add personalized details around the pictures, such as putting a green hat on an icon of the child or a briefcase in the father's hand. For those who have easy access to these and other symbols on the computer, stories can be quickly generated as situations arise. Alternatively, photographs can also be used, although this added step requires some extra work.

What if the child does not like doll play?

Some children respond better to actually acting out the event, or watching two or more adults acting out the event, rather than playing through it with dolls. For many children this is confusing ("You are not Joey! You are Mommy!"), while for others active and exciting physical re-enactment seems the most interesting. If you are really ambitious, two or more adults or siblings can act out a scenario and you can video-tape it, allowing the child to watch the video over and over.

What if the child gets carried away with the story and the undesirable behavior escalates?

Sometimes, when children first start acting out situations involving "naughty" behaviors, they are not sure how far they can take the play. When acting out aggression in play, they may actually begin to hit, or, if they are acting out becoming upset about a broken toy, they may actually break a toy. This is not uncommon and is part of the process of learning modulation of behavior and emotion. It is important to clearly and briefly move out of "play mode" when this happens. For example, if, when acting out hitting between dolls, the child really hits you, stop playing quickly, put on a serious look and say "No, no, just pretend." Then go back into playful mode, with smiles and silly voices signaling that you are playing. You may need to say, "This is just pretend hitting" several times. This will help the child understand and maintain the distinction. It will also show that actually doing the undesired behavior stops the fun, while pretending keeps it going. Usually, after a few instances of moving in and out of play, the child will understand.

Examples

These and all other examples are based on actual situations but have been altered to insure confidentiality.

Example I

Six-year-old Ellen has significant anxiety and is quite a perfectionist. She becomes overwhelmed with unhappiness, sometimes seeming to panic if something such as a piece of a toy breaks or gets lost. She got two new toy balloons and one broke. She began crying and jumping about as if she had just been seriously injured or stung by a bee. Her mother and the therapist calmed her down, talking softly about what had happened, going over the sequence of events, with emotions in our voices ("First we were just playing with the balloons and then BANG it POPPED so suddenly, like THIS."). The therapist demonstrated what had happened a few times, acting it out with quiet but exaggerated emotion. She calmed to watch, moving back to whimpering at the popping event each time but generally calming down. Later in the day, the therapist initiated playing out the whole scene again, this time adding various physical and verbal humorous elements (e.g. "The balloon popped so loud I jumped to the ceiling!" "It was such a mess there were pieces all over!"). This time, she took great delight in this, making big loud exploding sounds and exaggerating her pretend crying. She wanted to play it over and over. The next day, the therapist wrote a story with pictures for her, including the balloon popping with big red "sound lines" near her crying face, then new balloons and her happy face. She read the story many times over and acted it out with facial expressions and voices. She studied the pictures, trying to imitate the sketched expressions and going back frequently to the page of her crying and then the page of her being happy at the end.

Example 2

Five-year-old Michael becomes very upset when someone is angry. Recently, his mother and grandmother exchanged angry words over the air-conditioner setting. He covered his ears and cried. After he calmed, he remained very worried and repeatedly asked his grandmother if she was still angry. Hearing anger in any form, even though it was mild and not directed at him, was extremely upsetting for him. The therapist acted this story out with him, actually touching the very air conditioner where the event had occurred. At first the therapist acted out both roles, that of his mother and his grandmother, so he could see what was happening. Once he understood the game, he took great delight in playing the role of the grandmother touching the air conditioner and having the therapist, as his mother, say "NO." A few times, he got carried away with the play and actually turned the air conditioner off. The therapist stopped playing, moved his hand away from but near the knob and said "Just PRETEND," and then continued. He quickly stopped going for the button and continued pretending. He wanted to play this game many times over. The therapist then switched roles on him and touched it. At first he was confused, but with modeling he was then able to pretend to be angry, shake his finger and say, "NO!" He played this game on and off for many days, always with loud, angry yelling of "NO," then great shrieks of laughter as he ran away from the "angry" person. He also studied the picture story many times over. He finally grew tired of the game, although weeks later he would often greet the therapist with this favorite "story." His tolerance for his mother and grandmother disagreeing increased substantially.

PART II

Tailoring Replays for Children with Specific Problems

Part II provides techniques for tailoring and adapting the style and level of sophistication of Replays for use with children who are non-verbal and/or just beginning to understand pretend play, for children who have trouble sustaining play with an adult, for older children who may feel too old to be doing pretend, and for those who especially enjoy reading and writing.

4

Tailoring Replays for Younger or Less Verbal and Symbolic Children

The power of Thought. The magic of the Mind!

— Lord Byron

Children who have little language and only a rudimentary understanding of pretend may be baffled initially by Replays. They may not yet understand the sequence of events that takes place in their own experience, leading up to an upset, and the subsequent calming down. Sometimes, the upset is so intense it seems to take over the child's ability to process the rest of the experience – that is, the building up and calming down steps. For example, a child may feel that toothbrushing is dreadful, even painful. Merely seeing the toothbrush may set her off; however, she may not have processed all that is involved in the sequence of toothbrushing, such as which aspect is unpleasant, and that the toothbrushing horror does indeed have a predictable end point.

Further, the child may have built up an intense response to surrounding events, e.g. seeing the toothbrush or toothpaste or even being taken into the bathroom in the morning. So calm interactions with the objects involved or during the event itself may not be possible until the child has been desensitized to the surrounding objects and sequences. Children at this level of symbolic understanding don't yet have a full grasp of the connection between pretending and their actual experiences, although they may have learned some pretend schemas. For children at this level, a multi-modal approach is needed before and during the implementation of Replays. Many children who first seem baffled by Replays for these reasons can indeed develop a good understanding of them over time. It is well worth the time and effort, as once the child has mastered Replays for one type of event, he or she is very often able to generalize to other situations. This multi-modal approach will vary depending on the child's specific needs and responses but will typically include the following steps:

- Improve the child's understanding of the relationship between symbolic play and their own experiences.

- Desensitize the child to the surrounding events or places by pairing them with happy experiences.

- Help the child cognitively understand the sequence of events leading up to and following the dreaded cause of upset.

- Finally, begin to use Replays.

If you try all these steps and it still doesn't work and the child appears confused, she simply may not be developmentally ready for this approach. Nevertheless, the other steps will help in decreasing the related anxiety and provide an opportunity to begin to teach pretend play. As the child's skills emerge, it is worth trying again. Sometimes, a child who seems to show little understanding one month will suddenly catch on the next month, a few months later or the next year.

Jessie and the doctor – a multi-modal approach

Jessie, a five-year-old girl, with little speech and emerging symbolic play, was terrified to go to the doctor. Unfortunately, she had chronic ear infections, often with accompanying pain, and required frequent visits. She also needed follow up for several other medical issues, but her phobia around doctors had become so intense that her parents found themselves postponing visits, even canceling appointments entirely, because they couldn't bear the emotional distress they caused her. She was generally a happy and compliant child and did not have many other significant fears, but this one was very intense. It had become extreme, including screaming, crying, and clinging to her parents on entering the clinic parking lot. She had enough receptive language to know when her parents told her she would be going to the doctor, and would become plagued with fear and anxiety almost immediately.

Her mother attempted Replays with her, drawing her attention to a realistic-looking doll with ears, having the doll say "OUCH! HURTS" while pointing to her ears. Jessie showed great interest, so this approach seemed to be working. Jessie took the doll from her mother and made the sign for "Call/telephone." Her mother, knowing this familiar game of pretending to call the doctor on the phone, played along. This seemed like it was going to work. However, once her mother had "called," Jessie was done with the play. Each time her mother re-introduced the same scenario, Jessie brought the doll to her mother to call. Clearly this was a pretend play "script" she knew and liked, but it was not clear she connected it to her own impending visit or to her own fear.

Jessie's mother further experimented by more directly demonstrating the part of the experience that was frightening, to determine if she could understand through pretend. She got out the toy stethoscope and otoscope and put them to the doll's ears saying "OUCH! NO NO!" in an effort to highlight the key aspect of Jessie's fears. Again, Jessie watched with interest but without amusement or fear, and returned the doll to her mother to call the doctor, not understanding the play. She enjoyed the play, but to her the "game" was calling the doctor, not acting out being at the doctor's office. She wasn't avoiding the scene, for she watched with interest, but rather she demonstrated a lack of understanding.

Often when children on the autism spectrum are beginning to learn pretend play, they know a few familiar "scripts" from real life or a video. They may appear to have a greater understanding of the relationship between this pretend "script" and real life than they actually do. Jessie's inability to process the scene outside her "call on the phone" script suggested she needed more experience with pretend to further understand

and flexibly apply it to her own experiences without relying on a single script.

Jessie was not yet at the stage of understanding a sequence of pretend events and how they related to *her* reality. She had a few pretend scripts, which she could play through with dolls (e.g. dressing and undressing them, feeding them, and having her mother pretend to call the doctor). She greatly enjoyed playing these scripts over and over in the same way and, in fact, she would become frustrated at attempts to vary them. Her understanding of play was not yet at a reality-based, flexible, multi-step level, and, hence, she was not able to relate the out-of-context doctor scene to her own experiences.

When children have so many of the pre-requisite skills (rudimentary understanding of pretend; strong interest in watching pretend scenes; ability to anticipate scary, upcoming events), Replays can be effective. If these skills are lacking, Replays can also be effective but only after additional work with pre-requisite skills.

Jessie needed to learn two major components in order for Replays to work:

1. to have an internalized sense of the steps involved in a sequence of events, and

2. to be able to connect doll play with her real-life experiences: the doll represented her.

To work on the first goal, her mother took lots of pictures of event sequences, including the going-to-the-doctor sequence, and ordering these into two-, three-, and four-step photo stories. She chose components of events that were both easy to photograph and were particularly meaningful for Jessie. They took pictures of going to school in three steps (wake up, go in the car, meet the teachers at school), of going to bed in three steps (have dinner, take a bath, get tucked in), and then of going to the doctor (go in the car, crying while having ears checked, smiling on the way out in parent's arms).

The process of taking pictures and looking at them together took several weeks. This family used a digital camera and downloaded the pictures on the computer so they could show them as a "slide show" as well as printing them out in actual sequence. The picture sequences need not be fancy or professionally produced to be effective, however. Photographs can be taped into a small notebook, over the pictures of an old "board book," taped in order onto the refrigerator or other surface, or tacked onto a bulletin board. If you prefer, you can draw the pictures rather than using a camera. Simple drawings have certain advantages: the child can watch and "add" components as desired; you can make several variations on the same series to keep the child interested; and you can show greatly exaggerated emotions, such as an ear-to-ear smile or big blue tears.

Jessie took great interest in these mini-stories, showing them to her teachers at school and carrying them around the house. She especially liked carrying around the corresponding picture series: she took the going-to-bed series to bed and the going-to-school series to school. So the first mission, that of teaching her sequencing as it applied to her life, had been accomplished, at least at an elementary level, and that was sufficient for addressing her doctor fears in the same manner.

Often children can systematically be taught symbolic play and sequencing of events by pairing a doll or favorite figure both in space and time with their everyday events, over the course of days or weeks and across many situations. When a child eats breakfast, the doll eats breakfast; when the child puts on his or her pajamas and has a cup of milk before bed, the doll puts on its pajamas, too, and has a cup of milk before bed.

Next, Jessie's mother and teachers worked simultaneously on expanding her understanding of doll play, apart from her learned scripts. They paired everyday activities with a doll. A doll sat in her chair with her at meals; a doll bathed with her; a doll had its diaper changed when she did. When she fell down or got a bump, once comforted, the doll fell and was comforted too. At school, the doll joined the group at snack time and even for art projects. After a few weeks, she was increasingly initiating having the doll partake in her activities. She especially enjoyed the more dramatic activities such as diaper changes and falling down.

Once a child has recognized the doll is "like me" and "does things I do," demonstrations of, and ultimately participation in, multi-step sequences become easier to process. The child focuses on and plays through the sequence leading up to the upset, the upset itself and the calming down, much in the same way an adult will talk about and re-experience a painful event, or a typically developing child will use play to cope with dramatic or upsetting events.

Jessie's parents and teachers gradually increased the number of steps involved in these most interesting dramas. When initially the doll just fell down and was picked up, Jessie was not interested in drawing out the play. Over time, more detail was added: "Walk, walk, walking…then WHOOPS! Tripping…and BANG bumped her head" "OUCH! WAAAA, WAAA!…picking her up, giving her head a kiss…then resume WALK, walk, walk." She now had several multi-step sequences of doll play from her life. At times, she would revert to her old favorite: having Mommy call the doctor over and over, but often she was engaged with the new play sequences.

Finally, Jessie's understanding of doll play had reached a point at which she could play through going to the doctor, getting upset, having ears checked, calming down, and leaving the doctor. Jessie watched this with much greater involvement than initially, taking an increasing role as the doctor, as herself, and as the calming parent. She wanted to play the upset part over and over, which is usually a very good indication that the child has truly understood the play and is using it to practice coping with their own upset. This was a key "breakthrough" moment in the effective use of Replays in helping Jessie cope with her fears.

To reduce intense fears or phobias that the child has generalized across settings, implementing basic behaviorally based desensitization is a good complement for Replays. By pairing aspects of the fearful event with fun, positive emotions, one can help the child approach the actual event, as well as engage in play around the event, in a calmer state. For example, children with extreme reactions to toothbrushing, haircutting, nailclipping, taking medicine, etc. can be encouraged to play (with safe supervision) with toy versions of the instruments or utensils, or the instruments themselves, so the fear is not spread to actual or associated materials and locations (see also Chapter 8 on sensory-related fears).

Jessie's fear of the doctor had spread to the events leading up to the doctor visit. By the time she arrived at the doctor's office, she was in a state of severe distress and calming was no longer possible until the visit was over. So it was key to "desensitize" her to all the events surrounding the visit, so she would be in a state to cope with the actual encounter and examination by using what she was learning cognitively and emotionally through the Replays. To desensitize her, the family made several "just for fun" visits to the parking lot of both the doctor's office and the hospital, often with her brother along. They would explain they were just driving through and "no doctor today." But because of her limited language and intense emotional response, she did not initially understand. The first few times the family drove through the parking lot and then got ice cream or went to the park, Jessie would cry. Over time, she realized that they weren't going to see the doctor and stopped crying. Then her parents stopped the car, went into the clinic gift shop and bought some favorite stickers for Jessie and her brother. Jessie was anxious going in, but happy once she saw the gift shop and happy leaving. While this was time-consuming, it was far less stressful than dealing with her intense emotional reactions during actual doctor visits.

Jessie's teachers drew a simple five-page story of Jessie going to the doctor, with two pages in the middle reflecting upset. By this time, her understanding of picture sequences and the doctor event had advanced to the point where she could follow the story step-by-step. She again liked looking at the upset pages and making sad faces indicating that she was using the material in a way that would lead to better coping.

Unfortunately, before all the preparations of play and desensitization were complete, Jessie developed another ear infection and had to go to the doctor on short notice. Ideally there would have been a "well baby" check-up visit before this, many more opportunities to use the Replays and perhaps to make a complete Replays story book. But reality intruded. So Jessie's parents got out her doll and went through the Replays scene, although they had only run through it a few times during the past few days. Jessie watched, mimicked the adult voice tones

Jessie's ears hurt. OUCH! Mommy calls the doctor.

Jessie and Mommy drive to the doctor. Jessie is SCARED! NO DOCTOR!

Jessie and Mommy wait for the doctor. Jessie is VERY SCARED! NO NO DOCTOR!

The doctor checks Jessie's ears. OUCH! The doctor is DONE! Jessie is not scared any more!

The doctor visit is ALL DONE! Jessie and Mommy play bubbles! Jessie is VERY HAPPY.

of upset, then happiness, then checked the doll's ears and hugged her afterwards. They brought the doll and the otoscope to the doctor's office. Jessie was anxious but not crying in the parking lot, and her fears began to escalate, but were still manageable, in the waiting-room. She looked through the pictures of her "ice cream visit" as she waited, clutching her doll and sitting on her mother's lap. The doctor helped by calmly asking Jessie if she wanted her to check her doll's ears first, and Jessie held out her doll; Jessie was calming through this play. She cried when the doctor checked her ears, but was not as panicked as before, and she calmed quickly while still in the office.

This had been the most successful doctor's visit Jessie had ever had and it helped her parents feel more comfortable scheduling other necessary appointments. It also gave her a new script at the doctor's office, which led to many more positive experiences. While some appointments went better than others, she no longer had the pre-appointment panic in the parking lot, and hence it was usually possible to play through her fears and calm her more quickly during the visits. She continues to bring her Replays story book and her doll to doctor's appointments!

5

Tailoring Replays for Older, More Verbal Children

Fill your paper with the breathings of your heart.
— *William Wordsworth*

In general, Replays is most applicable for children at a stage in their development where they are just beginning to understand pretend play skills, through the stage in their development where they are "too cool for school" and will no longer readily enjoy engaging in pretend. This is often from about age 18 months or two years through to about age eight depending very much on the child's own development. Many children on the autism spectrum are late to begin pretending but enjoy it well into adolescence and beyond, as long as the right figures that are of prime interest are used. In this chapter, we present some "tricks" for adapting Replays for children who are developmentally beyond and without apparent interest in pretend play.

Sometimes older children might enjoy pretend but know they are supposed to be "too old" for it. Having pretend play figures, which the child might show interest in, lying around and available (e.g. superheroes, action figures, robots or "transformers," teen-oriented dolls, toy soldiers and other figures from the child's culture, including favorite TV shows or movies) will often entice older children to begin to engage in pretend play, especially if they don't think the adults are paying much attention. Once the child is happily playing with the figures, the adult can often enter the play with a similar figure.

Keeping the pretend Replays topic somewhat distant from the actual issue in content, although similar in theme, while keeping the play somewhat consistent with the actual figure's fictional characteristics, at least initially, can lure the child into the play and allow them to practice their fears, without even realizing it or objecting to it. For example, for a child who can't tolerate making mistakes, Superman® makes a mistake rescuing the wrong figure or train, and has to retrace his steps to figure it out again. For a child afraid of noises, the transformer robot can be terrified and quickly transform to a plane and fly away, upon hearing a "massive explosion" right next to him.

Sometimes children will become interested in the use of dramatic acting out of situations. Brief spontaneous improvised skits can be used as Replays to act out situations, related in theme to issues that are challenging for children. The goal within dramatic Replays is still to incorporate exaggerated playful responses to actual upsetting situations, rather than to teach appropriate behavior or act out correct responses. The child may pretend to be the teacher, coming up with extreme, unrealistic punishments while the adult playfully enacts the child's tiny misbehavior, for the child afraid of getting in trouble. Once children are fairly verbal and able to sustain focus for interactive drama, the field of drama therapy offers a great deal of material for varied uses of acting and drama games for helping children work on issues related to complex or disturbing emotions.

Co-writing

Some children, especially older children with sufficient language skills, and children who have advanced reading and writing skills (sometimes referred to as hyperlexic), enjoy the form of Replays we call co-writing. This technique is also particularly effective for good readers who have trouble staying on topic, and/or who have language processing or short-term memory problems. The advantage of co-writing is that the child's spoken words appear before them. The adult can use paper and pen or colored markers, or write at a computer screen when available.

While some children may initially want to write or type themselves, for this technique, the adult writing or typing, with the child "dictating" much of the time, is generally most effective. This is for several reasons. First, adults generally type or write more quickly and can keep up with the child's spoken words and thoughts, such that the typing process itself doesn't interfere with the flow of thought and interaction. Second, this allows the adult to have some control over what is written, over the direction of the story or expression, just as in the Replays the adult has control over the figures.

It is important to note that co-writing is very different from encouraging a child to have his own journal, which is just for his own words and expression, perhaps with adults responding on other pages or perhaps kept private, depending on the child's issues and needs. This is the same for symbolic play, when there are times to let the child control all the play and other times when adult direction is very useful for specific purposes. Co-writing is a child-centered but adult-led interactive activity incorporating the same principles as Replays, but in written instead of a pretend play medium. Some children, particularly those advanced enough to enjoy reading, but young enough to still pretend, enjoy both pretend Replays, using figures, as well as co-writing.

Seeing one's words appear seems very validating to many children, especially those who love the written word, as many children on the Asperger/autism spectrum do ("I FELT it, I SAID that, and there it is in PRINT!"). You have created an environment in which they are being listened to. Often children will smile during this process, watching as their sentences appear. Further, children will often want to stop and read back what they have created. This allows children to correct or revise if the adult has not expressed their words accurately or if they want to revise how they first expressed their thoughts or feelings. Additionally, this is helpful for children with attention and/or short-term memory problems, who have trouble staying on topic or remembering what they have said so far. Many children have difficulty with interactive topic maintenance as well as language processing, and are helped by this method to express coherent longer topical themes than they might be able to do verbally.

Adding visual drama

Colored markers and big blank pads afford room for creative expression such as huge letters or intense colors to express strong emotions. Sketches can be incorporated. A computer screen provides enormous flexibility in expression and changes of expression. For example, one can rapidly extend an angrily expressed "no" to

"NOOOOOOOOOOOOOOOOOOOOOOOOOOOO"

spreading powerfully across the screen, even filling the screen, simply by holding down the "o" key. The child might greatly enjoy this and even want a whole page of red, large-type "NO"s initially, but then, as he begins to calm and the process begins to take effect, might want to delete some or all of these. Similarly, expressions of more articulated feelings can be expressed in large type: "Yogurt makes me SICK TO MY STOMACH!!!! My little brother gets so much attention and I want to SCREAM!"

Alex who has Asperger's

Alex's psychologist did a series of co-writing sessions with Alex, a very bright ten-year-old with Asperger's syndrome in a regular class whose placement was at risk because he was having so many meltdowns around being corrected, making mistakes, having to do work over, etc. The teachers were aware of this problem (naturally!) and were quite accommodating in working around it, but Alex was smart enough to know when he made a mistake and some of the pressure to do work over at this point was self-imposed. The staff had also worked out a behavioral plan that Alex liked, through which he earned extra computer time for each period he was able to remain calm. These efforts had helped reduce his tantrums but had not eliminated them.

One day his teacher told him gently that he might want to look at problem #7 again. Later, the psychologist learned from his teacher that Alex had had a yelling tantrum and had to leave the room after realizing he had made a mistake. In Alex's psychology session, he narrated, in an upset but controlled voice, while the psychologist wrote, reflecting his emotions: "I DO NOT MAKE MISTAKES!!!! I HATE DOING WORK OVER!!! I WILL NEVER EVER EVER EVER EVER EVER DO WORK OVER!!!! ONCE IS ENOUGH. DOING WORK OVER MEANS DOING IT A HUNDRED MILLION BILLION GAZILLION GOOGLPLEX TIMES. 'ONCE IS *IT*', I SAY!"

Just as in the pretend play, in the co-writing session, the adult helps or allows the child to first express his or her own experience of the event. It can be very tempting, just as in the play, for the adult to interrupt this sort of flood of expression of frustration and begin to try to reason with the child ("Your teacher was just trying to help you learn the material; you just had to fix one little part, not the whole thing; everyone makes mistakes sometimes," etc.). Such comments are helpful at times, but during this activity the idea is to help the child express how it *feels to him or her* during these upsetting events. Similarly, during the pretend play the adult helps the child to first carry on about how dreadful it is to have one's teeth brushed or take medicine. This expression is the beginning process of re-experiencing the upset feeling in a calmer environment, mastering it and developing solutions to generalize in the real world.

As in pretend play, the adult, in Alex's case the psychologist, added her own angry words to his, but in a different color in case he felt she "got it wrong" so he wouldn't feel intruded upon: "DOING WORK OVER IS ANALOGOUS TO EATING A MEAL OVER! IT'S AN OUTRAGE! ONCE IS MORE THAN SUFFICIENT SOMETIMES."

She knew he enjoyed long and interesting words (e.g. "analogous"), and actor-like phrases (e.g. "it's an outrage") so she included these. She then added some humor as she felt he was becoming too upset to switch this around to a problem-solving point. She tried as in play to pair the dreadful feeling with a playful emotion. Again, she exploited his love of word play: "DOING WORK OVER IS THE MOST HORRIBLE, OUTRAGEOUS, ANGERAGOUS, SPRINDICULOUS, HORRIFICULOUS THING THERE IS."

He began to smile; then, after quickly informing her those were "not technically real words," he added a few of his own with increasing pleasure. He became more and more involved in this word list activity and she let him continue for some time. This was a calming and amusing activity for him, and provided both with a little break from the intensity of writing about his frustration. It also helped him feel a small and manageable amount of frustration without becoming consumed by it.

She ended this session with typing: "Well, SOMETIMES I MIGHT be willing to try to fix part of a problem. Maybe."

He added: "And maybe not. You just never know."

He did not ask her to delete this partial concession, and left the door open to the possibility of tolerance. She considered this substantial progress. At home, his father continued the activity in the same vein. His father, too, loved word games and they invented a whole page of made-up words to describe how it felt. He showed Alex some poetry that used this style and also introduced the wonderfully useful children's book *Alexander and the Terrible, No Good, Very Bad Day* (Viorst 1972).

Very often, as with the playing through of the tantrum or objecting phase of Replays, and once a child has had ample opportunity to express himself in this way for a time, the child either initiates or follows the adult's lead in working toward some kind of solution. The adult can begin to stimulate this process by saying "Well how about if I hand you a NEW problem 7 – you can do a FRESH one, rather than do that one over..." This may result in the child further expressing outrage, which may provide more information about what it is about doing work over that is so upsetting, as well as allowing the child to continue to express himself and be heard, but within an appropriate, relatively controlled, non-threatening situation.

With co-writing, the process is the most important aspect, just as with the pretend play, although after some sessions there will also be a printed-out product to read over later. Also, as with the pretend play version of Replays, the child will often want to co-write about the same issue or story over and over, which is part of the mastery component, making this an effective medium.

When using a computer screen, the process can be easier and more motivating by adjusting the font size and style to the child's preference. Smaller, younger, more fidgety children may stick with this longer if they sit on your lap as you type, while other children may wander about the room as they compose, checking back to the screen to see how their words are looking or to read back over a sentence. Pictures can easily be copied and pasted from software or the internet as well, such as "clip art" and other free downloads of pictures of angry children or children having haircuts, doing homework, etc. When searching picture databases, it is important either to be sure in advance the database is child-safe, such as from a children's software program, or, if it is a general picture site, such as Google Images, that the adult has pre-selected a variety of picture options, because images may pop up that are inappropriate for the child regardless of the search term typed in.

Reference

Viorst, J. (1972) *Alexander and the Terrible, No Good, Very Bad Day.* New York: Aladin Paperbacks.

6

Tailoring Replays for Active Children with Short Attention Spans

Energy and persistence alter all things.

— Benjamin Franklin

Many children with high activity levels, including those who have a diagnosis of attention deficit hyperactivity disorder (ADHD), may have an interest in Replays but may not be able to focus or stay in one place long enough to participate in and process a whole scenario. There are many "tricks" around this common challenge, including the following:

1. Organize seating that is both appealing and confining in order to provide sufficient structure such that, when attention veers, at least the body remains in one place. That way, a child is more likely to resume attention to the adult or activity again. Seating options include:

   i.   an adult-size armchair with a tray

   ii. an adult and child seated across from each other in chairs such that the adult can be playfully confining by virtually holding the child in his or her lap

   iii. a high chair or booster seat for toddlers

iv. a swing, with or without a tray top, at a playground or indoor gym. The adult can stand or sit on a big ball or chair in front of the child.

v. therapeutic seating, such as a Rifton chair, or a less expensive and more traditional-looking chair, which can often be found in toy stores or children's furniture stores

vi. try a rocking chair, bean bag chair or one with a movable cushion, and try various locations in the room, such as in a corner or facing a wall, rather than in the middle of the room.

In any confining set-up, the child must be safe and comfortable. While very active children don't like being confined, they may be more cooperative if it is introduced in a natural, playful fashion with favorite activities (e.g. bubbles; snacks; water play) and then moves into novel Replays. Over time, being confined will often become a signal that fun is about to begin. In fact, children who may have initially resisted will go to the "play chair" to indicate they want to play.

2. Use escape as the initial Replay for children who have some understanding of symbolic play. Parents can use this if they are trying to play in one room and the child keeps running off or "escaping" around the house. Therapists can use this approach in an office if a child is anxious and trying to get out the door during the first visit. For example, an Elmo or other popular favorite animal or doll can be held or captured as it is trying to leave the room. It is generally most effective to make this initial exposure quite dramatic to get the child's attention ("I WANT TO GO NOW!!!" says Elmo, kicking the door or pulling at the doorknob – or whatever the child is doing). For many children this becomes very interesting play, more interesting than escaping themselves, and they may bring Elmo over for repeated demonstrations. Hence, the initial Replay around wanting to leave is successful. However, a few minutes later, the child may become very active again and regaining her attention may still be a challenge.

3.   "Mini-Replays" such as these are often the most effective for beginning use of Replays with very active children. A tiny bit of the child's behavior can be instantly replayed with high emotion. The child spills his juice, so the doll spills his juice right after. The child eats cereal, so the doll tries to steal some too. This high-affect Replay performed very quickly so little attention is required will often be of great interest to even the most active child. From Mini-Replays one can often proceed to adding small steps, making them gradually longer and adding more complexity.

4.   Do "Active Replays." Run around to act out scenes, as long as the space is small enough so the child doesn't simply run out of interactive play range. A small fenced-in play yard, a carpeted playroom, living-room or kitchen cleared of dangerous, small or breakable objects can work well for Active Replays. While parks are often too big or busy, sometimes an empty, enclosed tennis court can be used, especially if the child has some sort of ride-on toy to slow her down. Challenges related to bolting, not listening and impulsivity, which are all common for active children, can all be played through using Active Replays. With more creativity, most challenges (e.g. fear of bees, bugs, dogs; not wanting to go to school or to go to any specific place; separation anxiety) can be played through actively on the go. Sometimes Active Replays are also useful for underaroused children and for those who are fearful and anxious, as the movement itself can raise arousal and decrease fearfulness.

Ben who was active and angry – an Active Replays example

Ben, an extremely active four-year-old with autism, often yelled at adults, children and even strangers, in a loud, angry-sounding voice. This may have been a combination of his general high state of arousal, and some anger that had developed, perhaps because he had been told "No" or "Stop it," so often. He had become quite mischievous about running away, and this was becoming a safety concern. His behaviorist had developed a plan to reward him for coming back and staying with his parents. They were beginning to practice brief outings together.

Ben's speech therapist was also interested in trying Replays. She made an initial attempt with dolls in her office, but he was not able to focus on pretend play. He spent most of the visit yelling "NO!" and trying to leave. She then tried using her outdoor playground space, although the pace was too slow to keep him engaged. Then she thought of using ride-in plastic toy cars, to both slow him down and keep him contained and accessible for interactive play. But he drove away to the other side of the playground. However, the speech therapist ignored him and he eventually drove back. She pretended to chase him as he drove away, hence getting some beginning interaction going. He smiled at first, then yelled angrily again.

Once this game was established, the therapist began to act out a very familiar scenario: Ben runs away and an adult calls him back in a loud and stern voice. In this safe, confined setting, HE could be in control. She pretended to be angry and shook her finger "No! no! – you stay here! Don't drive away!" and he laughed and drove off, only to return immediately to repeat the routine. He wanted to play this game over. The high activity level kept him focused, while the familiar theme amused and satisfied him. In addition, he sought out and sustained eye contact, sharing happy grins throughout the play. Over the course of several sessions, Ben and his therapist were able to engage in role reversal. That is, she would be Ben and run away, and he would yell for her to come back, a completely new role for him. This clearly demonstrated that he understood this interaction at a more sophisticated level.

Ben's parents played similar versions of this runaway and come back game with him at home. While the routine alone was not sufficient to teach him not to run away, it resulted in more satisfactory interactions with his family and decreased his overall anger; also, in combination with his behavioral plan, he learned to stay with his parents in many environments, only occasionally running off.

The speech therapist then drew a picture story. She made this a very active project as well, spreading paper across the floor. So after she drew him in his car, he "zoomed away bye bye" making a big red line with a crayon as he ran across the paper. After doing this in-between step several times, they made him a more traditional Replays story. Ben especially liked the picture with him in his car waving and the caption "BEN WANTS TO ZOOM AWAY! BYE BYE!" but also smiled at the "happy coming back page." The behaviorist joined in and created similar picture stories for dealing with other difficult situations such as running away at the grocery store and the local mall.

PART III

Replays for Specific Situations

7

Replays for Children just Discovering Mischief

The opportunity for doing mischief is found a hundred times a day, and of doing good once in a year.

— Voltaire

When children first discover mischief, this can be very upsetting for the adults involved, at least initially. A child who used to sit in a high chair and eat or sit at Circle Time and listen to the teacher, or who never before climbed on furniture or drew on walls, suddenly turns into a monster, deliberately disobeying and engaging in behaviors never observed before. For typically developing children, this often first happens in the first few years of life and is the basis for the disorder referred to as the "Terrible Twos." While children with autism spectrum disorder or other developmental disabilities may have behavioral problems at any point in development, this specific deliberate mischievous pattern of behavior can be seen as an important milestone in their development. Deliberately mischievous behavior involves a great deal of social perspective taking or what is sometimes called Theory of Mind – that is, children know what THEY want, know that what YOU want is different from what they want and, further, know how you will react when they do what they want that is different from what you want! Often when children with developmental disabilities first discover this amazing phenomenon they become especially highly motivated to test out their social hypotheses and see if they can indeed achieve the response in you that they anticipate as a result of doing what they think you don't want them to do. For some children, this can become virtually a full-time hobby, but fortunately there are many effective ways to work through this period of development.

Earlier in development, many children on the autism spectrum are not aware of or focused on noticing the social aspect of their behaviors, such as climbing on furniture or running around at mealtimes. Young children on the autism spectrum who engage in these behaviors, while perhaps aware they are not supposed to at some level, are not yet generally seeking a social response from you, but rather are focused on engaging in the desirable and fun activity. As children become more socially aware, they begin to notice and find it interesting that certain behaviors cause a strong emotional response in the adults or children around them, and they work hard as they research this further, trying variations on their initial behavior.

No doubt about Thomas

Thomas, a six-year-old with PDD, had generally followed along well with the classroom routine for several months of integrated kindergarten. One day during Circle Time, he saw something interesting in the hall outside the open classroom door. He left the circle and went out to look at it. A teacher followed him and told him to come back in, looking very upset and surprised. He came back, but the next day at Circle Time he did exactly the same thing, only this time he waited at the door, looking back to see if his teacher would come after him.

The key to figuring out if mischief is deliberately motivated by seeking a social response is the child's looking-back behavior, looking to the adult's face, smiling and making eye contact, or somehow making sure to bring the event to the adult's attention.

Getting the Max-imum reaction

Max, a generally well-behaved, happy, and highly energetic four-year-old with autism, had recently discovered he could scale the kitchen drawers and reach the cabinets above. This naturally brought a strong reaction from his father who was fearful for Max's safety. Max laughed when his father firmly told him to get down, then went right back up after his father had left the room. This time his father was not there to respond, but Max, who was not generally verbal called "DA-DA!," clearly working extra diligently to get his father's attention and reaction.

Max LOVES to climb. He is SO HAPPY climbing!

Daddy is mad. "NO, MAX! COME DOWN RIGHT NOW!"

Max is MAD. "NO, DADDY! I WANT TO CLIMB!"

Daddy and Max have a snack. Max is happy again. Daddy is happy again!

Often when a child discovers this interactive mischief through one behavior or in one situation, he is quickly able to generalize and experiment in many situations. It is interesting to observe that children who have so much difficulty generalizing many other skills can quickly generalize mischief, perhaps because it is so emotionally exciting and interesting. For some children, this pattern is the first time they have figured out a way to predictably and successfully achieve social engagement, which, although it is negative, may feel extra good compared to their earlier social deficits. Finally, the child has found an intense social game he has full control over, is always successful at, and fully understands.

Soon after discovering that running out of the room during Circle Time always led to his teacher following with amusing expressions on her face, Thomas, the six-year-old mentioned earlier, began being mischievous in many different ways at home and at school, doing things he had never done before. At school, he began painting on the walls, knocking over other children's block buildings, and at home he began turning over the food served to him at the table. Parents and teachers were initially frantic, believing that he was regressing, and brought him to his neurologist who did not see any concerning findings because his language and motor skills were continuing to develop, and he also seemed quite happy. The school sought the help of a behavioral consultant, and she was able to see the mischief pattern in full force. She set up a positive behavioral plan such that Thomas earned puzzle pieces that added up to computer time for staying with the group at circle and playing appropriately in the block area, picking two behaviors to focus on. She also stressed that his teachers and parents should not show a big reaction when righting something he had spilled or bringing him back to the group. She suggested simply removing toys or food that he threw on the floor and giving him other options after a few minutes. These strategies were helpful in reducing these behaviors, but Thomas quickly discovered new ones.

The consultant then suggested doing Replays with Thomas at home and at school. At home, Thomas liked to play with his three-year-old sister and they had begun doing some very basic pretend together. The consultant and his mother set up a pretend meal time with their play kitchen set. Once everyone was seated, the consultant said "UH OH" and slowly threw her pretend food on the floor. Thomas and his sister watched with great surprise never having seen an adult play in this way. His sister said "NO! NO!" and put the food back on the plate. The consultant then playfully said "UH OH" and very slowly began pushing her food to the edge of the table. Thomas laughed and pushed it off the edge for her so it landed on the floor. His sister again said "NO NO." So Thomas now seemed to understand the play, as did his sister, who was also witness to this at mealtimes. Thomas' sister then pushed her food on the floor and looked up at the consultant. She was hoping Thomas would say "NO!" but he was watching her too, so this time the consultant said "NO! NO!" and put the food back. Thomas' mother then said "UH OH!" and began to very slowly push HER food on the floor. She slowed down the play, as had the consultant, hoping Thomas would "step in." Thomas leapt up saying "NO, Mamma!" pushing the food back onto her plate. "NO THROW FOOD, MAMMA!" he said. She began with "UH OH" a few more times and then they each took turns saying "UH OH," starting to push the food off the plate and one of them would say "NO!"

In this play, Thomas could get a lot of practice with his new discovery of mischief, without having to actually engage in real mischief. The consultant had the list of behaviors he had been doing at school, and they were able to play through several of these at home because the nature of the behaviors made them unamenable to play within the classroom setting.

His mother got paintbrushes with no paint and they took turns pretending to paint colors all over the wall while the other said "NO PAINTING ON THE WALL! YOU NEED TIME OUT!" Thomas was easily able to generalize this to doll play and they played knocking over block structures as the other children got angry. His mother, the consultant, and his sister also role-played running out of the room at Circle Time, with the teacher racing after him. This was one of Thomas' favorites, perhaps due to the real chase that ensued each time. He was able to play both the weary teacher saying "GET BACK HERE RIGHT

NOW!" to his mother, the consultant and his sister, as well as, of course, playing the mischievous child. The consultant then also incorporated the behavior plan into the play such that whoever stayed at the circle got a pretend puzzle piece and was told "You're earning your computer time!"

While Thomas greatly enjoyed this theme of play for several weeks, his actual mischief declined quite quickly at home and at school. Fortunately, his sister also enjoyed this, as do most three-year-olds; so the two played mischief, one of their best interactive games to date, over and over, with their mother now and then giving them new ideas from one or the other's behaviors.

Elmo to the rescue

Max, the four-year-old with autism continued to engage in mischievous climbing – on tables, cabinets, the back of the sofa, and any furniture in his environment. He was very active and agile, and this was truly a fun activity for him, in addition to receiving attention from an adult. His father had tried all the basic behavioral techniques and just found himself continually pulling Max off high places as soon as he emerged from "time out." Max had little language or pretend play but his father decided to try "Instant Replays," pairing his favorite Elmo doll with his activity. Max climbed on the table, his father pulled him down and, while still holding him, had Elmo climb up just as Max had. His father then said "NO NO!" and pulled Elmo down but had Elmo instantly climb back up. The fast pace and new yet oh-so-familiar play held Max's interest. Max grabbed Elmo and made him climb up and looked to his father who cooperated, saying "NO NO" and pulled him off the table. Max then made Elmo climb on the countertop; and Max also told him "NO NO!," assuming both roles.

Max caught on to this play very quickly even though he had not engaged in pretend before. The pairing of the behavior with his own, and the frequency and intensity with which he had been climbing helped him make sense of this theme. He also got to enjoy exploring mischief over and over without actually being mischievous. He still loved to climb, so this play didn't fix the problem, but it stopped the intensity of it. Max's father also created a special area in the living-room by putting a mattress on the floor and several big cushions from an old couch together so he could redirect Max to a safe climbing place. He also made sure he got him to the playground as often as possible. At the playground they played chase a lot, with Max's father catching him, saying "I'M GOING TO GET YOU" or "I GOT YOU!" or something else with a mischief component to it. Max was able to extend his Elmo play to other characters and new scenarios, and this series of activities marked the emergence of Max's symbolic play skills.

The power of "NO!"

Like discovering mischief, discovering the power of "NO!" is an exciting and highly motivating event for a child. However, it can be very disruptive to everyone else! Often when children first discover they can indicate "no" either verbally or through signing "all done" or shaking their head, they use this frequently. "No" is typically learned well before "Yes," because it is far more motivating. One advantage is that this can considerably reduce behavioral manifestations for expressing "no," such as tantruming or throwing objects or running away. Many children in this stage of discovery use all their "no" means at once, pushing something away, saying "No, no" and signing and saying "All done!" for emphasis. These aspects of the development of "no" are similar for typically developing children, but can be more extreme and intense for children with significant communication disorders who may have little else that they can predictably communicate. This may be the most powerful social communication act they have experienced.

Often when children begin to use "no" in this over-generalized way, they may not truly mean "no" to what you are asking or offering, but they may mean "No, don't tell me what to do – I'LL be the one to decide that!" For example, an initial "no" or gesture for "all done," may be followed by a reaching for the very thing that was initially refused. Typically developing children in this stage often answer automatically "no" to anything asked, and then think about it and give their "real" response (Adult: "Do you want to play outside?" Child: "NO! (pause) Play outside (pointing to door)!"). Children with communication disorders may also do this but they may get more "stuck" at the refusal part of the interaction, not yet able to shift gears or process and respond quickly in two ways at once. Children who have previously been cooperative and interested in a variety of toys may suddenly begin to refuse everything "just because they can." Fortunately, there are many ways to deal with this, and it is perhaps most helpful for the adults to keep in mind that this reflects true developmental progress, and that like other developmental phases "this too shall pass."

To reinforce the child's communicative efforts and to help him or her feel "heard" and ultimately decrease the intensity, respond to the "no" when appropriate. However, it is also important for the child not to refuse everything! Offering choices is a wonderful strategy to give the child a greater sense of control and many opportunities to say "no," but, when the child refuses all options regularly, other means are necessary. One can initially validate the "no" verbally, then keep going regardless. For example, in response to a child who needs to get dressed pushing all clothes away saying "No," the adult can stop struggling and, mirroring the child's emotions and expanding their communication, say "NO! You DON'T want clothes on" indicating she understands the child, and following that with "But we HAVE to get dressed" and continue dressing the child. While the child may not understand the words, he may realize that his emotions were responded to. This may not stop the "no" but it may decrease the intensity.

Replays can be very helpful and fun for this stage. A doll or figure can be seated at the table and say "NO! YUCKY" and throw everything offered into a pretend garbage can. The adult can pretend to try to dress the doll who says "NO!" throwing each piece of clothing on the floor. Most children at this stage find this amusing and will keep handing back the items for a repeat performance. The doll can adamantly refuse plastic food representing the child's favorites, e.g. cookies or candy. If the child is signing, have the doll sign "All done" while saying it. Ultimately model an ending in which the doll chooses something that is fun/tastes good/feels warm to wear, and then allow the child to go back to requesting more "no" play. Children at the height of this stage may want to play the "no" game endlessly.

There is nothing wrong with taking breaks! But keep in mind that, generally, the more times the child plays through "no," the more likely he or she will get satiated and eventually tire of this fun new "game" in real life!

Short picture stories of "NO" can also be very appealing and helpful for practicing at this stage:

1. Mommy is putting Jack's shirt on.

2. Jack says "NO SHIRT!"

3. Mommy is putting Jack's pants on.

4. Jack says "NO PANTS!"

5. Mommy is putting Jack's shoes on.

6. Jack says "NO SHOES!"

7. Jack is getting COLD! Jack wants to go out and play.

8. Jack says "SHOES ON!"

9. Jack says "PANTS ON!"

10. Jack says "SHIRT ON!"

11. Jack is happy and goes out to play.

8

Replays for Sensory-related Fears and Anxieties

He who is not everyday conquering some fear has not learned the secret of life.

— *Ralph Waldo Emerson*

Many children with anxiety and/or on the autism spectrum have significant sensory over-reactivity. Some children are especially reactive to touch-related experiences. These children may become very upset or have meltdowns in response to haircuts, fingernail cutting, teeth-brushing or ear checks at the doctors. They may also dislike wearing specific clothes such as clothes with buttons, collars or tags, wearing glasses, bandaids or hearing aids, wearing shoes, diaper changes, being touched/bumped or kissed even by parents (some children "wipe it off") and may also be very picky eaters with strong food aversions. Some children are over-reactive to noise-related experiences such as school bells, people laughing all at once such as at a party, singing "Happy Birthday," to blenders or fans, thunder storms, hearing a baby cry, balloons popping, and fire alarms. Sometimes fears have multiple sensory and emotional components such as toilet training aversion, fear of bugs, dogs, taking medicine, having shots and doctors.

Some children have quite specific fears that are more complex, and likely have multiple origins, but that nevertheless are very predictable and hence can be worked with effectively. Fear of dolls or toys that "talk" or can be moved remotely or with switches (and these days it's the rare doll that doesn't do something), fear around certain parts in videos, and fear of expression of certain negative emotions (e.g. hearing "NO," or that someone is mad, in real life or even in a story or on TV) can all be addressed with Replays.

Often anticipation of these events is as upsetting or even more so than the events themselves. Many parents develop the strategy of not telling their child of a potentially anxiety-provoking event until just before it happens to prevent the child from worrying about it days before it occurs. In fact, families often develop a strategy of avoiding all talk related to the "issues" (e.g. haircuts) except for right before they occur. While this does prevent the anxiety build up over time, it eliminates opportunity for practice and mastery of the aversive event.

Often circumstances naturally surrounding these events also become "contaminated." For example, fear of balloons popping can lead to fear of seeing balloons, which can lead to fear of birthday parties, cakes, fairs, etc. Fear of bugs can lead to fear of going out at all. Fear of fire drills can lead to fear of going to school. Fears around certain parts of TV shows or videos can lead to fear of TV in general (which may not be a bad thing), but which in turn can lead to fear of going places where there might be a TV.

Through Replays, much of the extra anxiety and agitation around an event or issue can be eliminated. We think this is because the process that originally caused the strong reaction, such as an over-reactive or immature nervous system, when the child was younger, is often much less vulnerable than when the child first experienced the event. Since that time the child has "learned" to anticipate a strong reaction, and indeed then experiences it strongly and negatively and never "re-learns" that it is no longer so physiologically or emotionally unpleasant. For example, a child at two having his first haircut may have had very significant sensory sensitivities and may have been frightened by the whole event. Each haircut then becomes something to fear in advance; seeing the set-up, the child becomes filled with anxiety and, by the time the actual dreaded haircut occurs, he has built up a high level of agitation and experiences as a crisis what may now be only mildly physically unpleasant.

When Replays are effective, the child still may not like the event, but the extreme aspect of the reaction, that is, the component that was likely originally caused by physiological distress but then became a learned emotional response, can often be greatly reduced or even eliminated, much to everyone's relief. Sometimes the child then has so much pride from "conquering" his fear and/or gets so much good feedback that he may develop a liking of the event.

Below we describe Replays with Sam, who had developed a response of high resistance with rage in response to having his shoes put on, and another child, Mikey, who absolutely could not tolerate haircuts. We describe these in some detail to illustrate how Replays can be developed and refined for individual children. Replays can be developed in a similar fashion for issues of children resistant to taking medicine, to brushing their teeth, to dressing, or to having nails clipped. Dolls or action figures can spit out pretend medicine with the real medicine spoon, can throw a real toothbrush to the floor, can toss off clothing carefully put on, and pull their hands or paws away in fear from nail clipping, all with humor, playful exaggeration and repetition, and tinkering to suit the specific child's fears and reactions.

Three-year-old Sam, non-verbal, with mild PDD, who hated wearing shoes

Three-year-old Sam hated wearing shoes. He had many sensory issues, only agreeing to wear loose shirts and sweatpants. This was fine, as his parents found him appropriate clothes, mainly sweatpants and sweatshirts, that he could tolerate. His parents were also fine with his going barefoot or just wearing socks in the house, and taking his shoes off once they got to wherever they were going. However, whenever the family went out, or left a place, or when he played outside, which he loved doing, he would predictably have a tantrum about putting his shoes on. This had been going on since he first started walking, at

18 months. Sam had only a few words, so it was hard to reason with him. He also had little pretend play, so neither he nor his parents thought to act this out as a way to "practice." It had gotten to the point where, when the family brought out his shoes, he began to cry, and each time putting them on was a physical struggle. He received occupational therapy services as part of his school program, and the occupational therapist (OT) had tried many techniques for desensitizing him to touch. He had grown in many ways, now liking lotion and play with shaving cream and putty, which originally made him gag. However battles around shoes continued.

His OT decided to try Replays even though Sam did not engage in pretending. She took his shoes out of the stroller one session. He started to cry. However, she put them immediately on a boy doll. Sam watched curiously. She then had the doll quickly say in a loud silly-mad voice "NO NO NO SHOES!" and kick off the shoes onto the floor just as Sam usually did. Sam laughed and began excitedly jumping up and down. The OT demonstrated again, this time waiting a moment before starting the doll's "tantrum," and having it build up more gradually, saying more quietly "No…no" and then escalating to "NO SHOES" and kicking them off.

For children who are just beginning to understand the concept of pretend, but who greatly enjoy the high display of emotion of the "tantrum," slowing down the sequence of the playing through of the event (shoes on) to the upset/tantrum motivates the child to increase the pace, to get you to the "climactic moment" of the exciting tantrum. As the child figures out ways to "hurry you up" – for example, by vocalizing or saying "No no," he or she gradually becomes more of an active participant.

This time, Sam brought one of the shoes back over and handed it to the OT. She put it on the boy doll again and Sam immediately began making "OOOOOO!" sounds, his approximation for "No," and laughing. The OT then put the doll in Sam's hand and began to put the shoe on it. Sam shook the doll saying "OOOOO!," recreating the tantrum again while laughing.

Increasingly, Sam was taking an active role in the Replays, which both indicated he understood them and also meant his Replays experience was more like the "real thing."

Sam wanted to play this game about 15 times in a ten-minute period, each time the same way. The OT varied it a bit to increase the likelihood he would generalize the game to his own experience, by having the doll sometimes kick the shoes off, sometimes throw them off with its arms, sometimes just say "NO!" He enjoyed each of these variations.

Once it is clear from the child's response that he finds the play interesting and amusing, it is important to keep varying it slightly to increase the likelihood he will generalize it to his own experience, and, for some children, to prevent the game from becoming an entertaining but perseverative loop less and less tied to actual experience.

The OT tried to vary it further by having other dolls put the shoes on, wanting to make sure he was generalizing the symbolic component, but Sam only wanted to play the game with the same doll, reflecting his still fragile understanding of pretend. Every once in a while he took a brief break from the play, going over to play with a favorite cause-and-effect toy. Then he would spy his shoe on the floor or the doll, smile, and bring the shoe back to the OT for another round. The OT let him do this, only resuming the Replay when Sam initiated it.

Sometimes Replays are so intense and exciting for children that, while they are drawn to the play, they also need breaks from the level of emotional intensity it creates in them. Some children take small breaks and resume the play while others enjoy just a few "rounds" at a time, and will once again become engaged in the play at a later point in the day. If the child seemed to like the Replays, stops doing it, and doesn't resume it, the adult can explore if he or she really wants to do it but is not sure how to communicate his or her desire to restart, by starting again. If the child is no longer interested, trying later, perhaps with a different version of the play, is generally effective.

Finally, Sam seemed to have had enough of the game and moved on to other activities, seeming to become "satiated" for the time being. Sam's mother and the OT continued to talk about the approach. After about five minutes, Sam got his shoes, sat down on the floor, and for the first time tried to put his shoes on. He didn't have the motor skills to do this independently, so his mother sat down to help him and he calmly held his foot up for her to do this. He then reached up to hug his mother, who was also very pleased, both seemingly aware of the triumphant "battle" they had won!

Six-year-old Mikey with a diagnosis of autism who hated haircuts

Six-year-old Mikey hated haircuts. As a toddler his mother had cut his hair and he hadn't minded it, but he hated his first trip to the barber at around three-years-old, even though his father had gone and had sat in the chair with him. He had cried all the way through it, trying to wrench away, and as he got older and more aware he seemed to find haircuts more and more unpleasant. His agitation had spread such that he would become fearful and angry even if his mother or father tried to cut his hair. They had tried different electric devices but the noise of these seemed even more upsetting to Mikey. His parents had resorted to cutting a few strands at a time when he was sleeping, but this left him with a week of unusual looking haircuts, and they worried it wasn't fully safe, as he might twitch in his sleep or wake up. They had tried letting it grow long, but he also hated having it brushed, and his thick unruly hair was always full of tangles. His parents tried to bribe him with special candy or toys after a haircut, but it wasn't clear he under-stood this, and it wasn't powerful enough to keep him from becoming very agitated as soon as they either approached the barber shop, or his parents got out the haircutting machine at home.

Agitation around haircuts is very common in children with height-ened sensory sensitivities, including many children on the autism spectrum. Sensitivity around the head and ear areas are common. Fears around the actual cutting off of something can also play a part, and then the "whole body" experience of having to stay very still, together with adult mild stress, especially if scissors are used, around the danger, all combine to make this a common dreadful experience. Also, because it only happens relatively infrequently, typically once it is over, all involved heave a sigh of relief and the subject isn't raised again until a few months later when, once again, it's time for another traumatic haircut. Hence, the child does not get to experience frequent "practice" and the natural desensitization that can sometimes occur with this.

That there was a strong sensory component was clear as Mikey also hated wearing hats, hoods, sunglasses, and headphones, as well as teeth-brushing, hair brushing, face washing, and nose blowing. His school team had worked to desensitize his head and mouth area to touch through a variety of sensory experiences, which he enjoyed, and the family also tried to playfully touch around his head area when he was engaged in rough and tumble play with them. This helped somewhat, but his agitation around haircuts seemed to worsen and be more difficult to manage the older he became.

Mikey's parents began to do Replays. Mikey had emerging pretend play, having learned to feed Winnie the Pooh and put him to bed. He occasionally did this spontaneously. He also loved his toy cars. While he often lined these up, occasionally he would push them and make car noises. His parents decided to start Replays very concretely, with his mother pretending to cut his father's hair, while his father had a pretend tantrum. They picked a time when they were all seated at the table during dinner so Mikey would be a captive audience. First, they used big pretend scissors from a doctor kit, so Mikey wouldn't think he was really going to have a haircut. His mother said "Sit still, Daddy. Time for your haircut," holding out the towel and scissors. His father made a playful angry face and pushed the scissors away saying "NO haircut." Mikey looked a little alarmed. His mother tried it again and this time his father made his "tantrum" even more playful saying "Yucky haircut" and laughing, without pushing the scissors away. Mikey smiled and looked to his mother, who repeated "Time for your haircut, Daddy." This time, his father increased the pretend anger component, now that Mikey had tolerated the more playful version. "NO! Hate haircuts" and his father started to kick his legs and wiggle out of his chair. "Sit still, Daddy." His mother approached his father's (bald!) head and began to snip. Mikey said "NO, NO!" and laughed. His father took his cue and repeated this. After several times of playing this, his father said "OK, you can cut my hair. But I want CANDY!" His mother got a candy and gave it to his father and then pretended to cut his hair, while his father sat still and tolerated the haircut, but made silly angry faces and noises.

It is always tricky to know when to "resolve" the Replays and have the character accept or even enjoy the dreaded situation. Adults typically want to resolve it far sooner than the children. It can feel "wrong" to keep playing the tantrum or other undesired behavior over and over, as if one is "teaching" the wrong thing. However, of course the adult is only re-enacting behaviors drawn from the child's current frequently used "library" of behaviors, not teaching new behaviors. It is important to remember that, almost always, the child knows what he is supposed to do, but needs to play through his own unpleasant experience of the situation until he has "maxed out" and can only then enjoy completing the play correctly with the desired resolution or engaging in the activity with less upset. The child in fact may never want to do the play "correctly" with the desired resolution. That doesn't matter, as long as the child's experience of the real-life actual experience becomes more tolerable. Adding the candy reward at the end was motivating for Mikey to sometimes reach the point of tolerating the actual haircut part of the haircut Replay, although this wouldn't be necessary or helpful for some children.

After watching his father tolerate the haircut for a minute or so, Mikey then reached for the toy scissors from his mother and went to cut his father's hair, most likely wanting to re-initiate his father's playful tantrum. His father had a playful tantrum and Mikey laughed hysterically. He loved creating this effect using this familiar theme! After many Replays with him cutting each of his parent's hair, he then gave the scissors to his father and sat while his father pretended to cut Mikey's hair. He pretended to have tantrums with great gusto. After several rounds of this, Mikey wanted to go play in the other room. His parents sketched a simple two-picture haircut story. In the first picture, his mother was approaching him with the scissors and he was looking very mad. In the second picture, she was cutting his hair and he was smiling, with candy showing in his mouth. Mikey of course liked looking at the "mad" picture as well as the candy.

The family played this game several times throughout the week before Mikey's haircut, extending it to Winnie the Pooh as well. Finally, the time came to cut his hair, and they began with play, with the real scissors on Daddy and Pooh, then Mikey held Pooh and tolerated the actual haircut for a few minutes. He then began to look unhappy, and his mother stopped right away, giving him candy and praising him for sitting. It was several weeks before he could tolerate longer periods, with gradual increased tolerance each time. After a few more Replays, he sat back down and tolerated more of the real haircut.

Nine-year-old Alana with Asperger's, afraid of bugs

Children with heightened sound sensitivity and an overall high level of anxiety may develop fears about various environmental sound-producing stimuli including fire alarms, thunder, trucks backing up, dogs barking, or bugs. As an example, we will describe Alana, a nine-year-old with Asperger's and a quite disabling fear of bugs. In seasonal climates, this can peak when bugs start reappearing in the spring. For many children, the combination of the unpleasant buzzing sound, the unpredictability of their presence (e.g. suddenly flying into the child's face or ear) and, for some children, the associated biting element, all contribute to this common fear. While a slight fear of bugs is generally not problematic and children can simply be reassured, or get caught up in outdoor play and not be bothered anymore, in children prone to anxiety, this can spread to not wanting to go where there might be bugs, including not wanting to go outside.

Alana, a nine-year-old girl with Asperger's, had been fairly anxious since infancy, but this had faded out to some extent in her preschool years. However, several changes, including moving homes, entering "real" school and increasing awareness of her environment seemed to have caused a higher baseline level of anxiety. In April as the bugs were starting to appear, she was very bothered one day when one flew into her ear. She yelled and cried "Go away buzzy thing!", running to her mother. Her mother taught her to simply say "Shoo fly," teaching her the song as well. This was interesting to her and she was able to pretend this when there were no bugs, but she continued to shriek and run to her mother if she saw a real bug.

For some children and some kinds of fears, a simple algorithm or script can be reassuring, give the child a sense of control while giving them something else to think about, and be sufficient to eliminate the fear response. However, for more intense fears, practice with some level of actually experiencing the fear is needed in order to diminish it.

Alana didn't have any toy bugs so it was not easy to play pretend realistically. Her mother drew a bug, cut it out and had it pretend to buzz around her own ear saying "Go away bug! Shoo fly!" Alana enjoyed this play as well, making the paper bug buzz around her mother, as they engaged in Replays, but it didn't help the actual fear, which had now extended to her asking as she entered any new room "Any buzzy bugs in here?" It seemed the paper bugs didn't create enough of a sense of the fear response to help Alana practice mastering it through play. Her mother asked her teacher if there were any bug sets at school. Her teacher was able to get a set of quite realistic-looking plastic bugs for her to borrow from the elementary science teacher.

When props of the feared objects aren't realistic enough, they may not work for Replays because either a) the child may not make the connection between the props and the real objects, or b) as in Alana's situation, the prop may not be real enough to induce the small dose of fear needed to make the Replays involve experiencing and then mastering the fear. However, if they are too realistic, they may create too much fear to make a playful format possible. For example, using a real bug would clearly be too scary for Alana at this point, apart from the impracticalities! When using fairly realistic props for Replays around sensory or other fears, it is important first to desensitize the child to the actual prop through an initial warm-up phase of playful engagement with the prop itself.

Alana's mother put the fairly realistic-looking toy bugs into a paper bag. She first did some familiar fun bubble play with Alana to get her in a relaxed happy state. She then told Alana she had borrowed some toy bugs from her teacher, holding up the paper bag. Alana looked fearful and moved across the room, holding her blanky. Alana's mother knew she had to proceed very slowly giving Alana a lot of control as she worked to initially desensitize her. She pulled out one of the toy bugs and hid it in her hand so that Alana couldn't see it. She tried to peak Alana's curiosity. "You want to see this little toy red bug?" Alana nodded her head but stayed across the room clutching her blanky. Alana's mother very quickly opened and closed her hand showing Alana only a quick glimpse of the bug, both to get her more curious, and also to make sure not to overload her. Alana laughed saying "I can't SEE it!" Her mother did the same thing again. This time she showed it to Alana's nearby Barbie® very quickly in the same way, and had Barbie® too say in a squeaky Barbie® voice "I can't SEE it!"

For children like Alana with a good understanding of pretend, having a character join even the desensitization part of the play as a "third party" gives the child many possible ways to enter the play, and allows for more variations.

Now Alana approached her mother, trying to open her hand up. "What do you want?" her mother asked playfully, making sure Alana felt fully in control of the first viewing of the realistic bug. "I want to SEE it, Mommy!" Alana's mother opened her hand up and Alana looked at the bug with interest, not touching it. Her mother then showed it to Barbie® "See Barbie®, it's red and has spots." Her mother appealed to Alana's love of reporting visual detail. She then had Barbie® touch the bug just for a second and take her hand away saying "Ewww a buzzy bug!" Alana said "I want to touch it too" and she imitated Barbie®, touching it for just a second, saying "Ewww, a buzzy bug!"

Often children are very interested in getting to know more about the feared object but have no way of doing this as they are too afraid to begin. Alana's interest in the toy bugs was becoming stronger than her fear through the gradual play. She was almost ready to move to more exploration, and her mother gave her a script that allowed her to explore it further by touching it, while expressing her fear in a playful way.

Alana's mother also appealed to her daughter's love of categorization systems, and while her mother initially did not know much about bugs, they began to explore bug types, searching images on the internet.

Alana found this as fascinating as she had found dinosaur types and properties, Pokemon systems, and the solar system, in earlier phases. Her mother bought her a field guide to insects which she was also fascinated with, quickly learning various categories and properties. Alana's interest in bugs increased dramatically although her fears continued. This created a sometimes frustrating situation for her, as she wanted to study bugs but did not want to approach them or go outside where she might actually see them.

Once Alana had become desensitized to the toy bugs through a lot of Barbie® and bug play, and had in fact identified most of them through her field guide and the internet, her mother began Replays. She began incorporating the auditory and unexpected quality of bugs, as well as Alana's fear response. She began by tying a string to a toy bug and showing Alana how it could pretend to "fly." Alana reverted to reciting the facts about the bug that she and her mother had by now talked about many times, and which Alana had quickly absorbed with precision and delight, practically reciting from the website ("Mommy, that's a Dragon Fly in the Odonata family. The Odonata's habitats are USUALLY ponds, and they feed on insects"), indicating she had some level of raised anxiety by seeing this. Her mother let her go through this routine, then made the bug fly by Barbie® again, using the scientific words Alana had learned, saying "Lookout Barbie®, here comes the Odonata bug that eats insects and it says 'bzzzzzzzzzzz.'" Alana laughed, maybe at this mix of silly and factual play, maybe with the pleasure of hearing her mother use the terms she was currently taken with in the context of this play, and she was no longer scared. She had her mother attach each bug to the string and made it fly by Barbie®'s ear as she recited its name and properties. Her mother had Barbie® be a little scared each time.

Now that Alana was desensitized to the toy bugs and had her own repertoire of facts through which to systematize the bugs she was well armed to begin Replays to master her fears. She played Barbie®, scared by each bug in turn, and then her mother encouraged her to have them go by her mother's ear, land on her mother's hair, etc. Alana enjoyed watching her mother "SHOO" off the bugs, while she, Alana, said

"Don't be scared, Mommy, that's just a Dragon Fly, remember? The pond ones!" Finally, Alana was able to let her mother buzz the bugs around her ears, land on her hair and arms, and even allow all the bugs to be on her, laughing and trying to keep up with naming and categorizing as her mother added more and more to her pile. They played this game many times with many variations, and gradually Alana's fear of bugs diminished. Within a few weeks, she stopped asking if there were bugs as she entered a room, and was once again happy to go outside to play. When a bug came near her, she often announced what kind she thought it was and its properties.

9

Replays for Anxiety, including Obsessive Issues, Birthday Party Fears, and other Fears or Phobias

Nothing in life is to be feared. It is only to be understood.

— Marie Curie

Obsessive-compulsive-related fears

Many children have challenges around a certain sort of "perfectionism," or what some might call an obsessive or compulsive disorder (OCD). They may be quite anxious, and even minor violations of their sense of order or their perception of how things should be are experienced as extremely traumatic. Lining up for recess, a child with this issue might break down in tears, or become aggressive if he is not first. Some children find a way to cope by being last, which is more often allowed! Losing in a game, or in a perceived competition, such as racing to the school or car door, may be devastating enough to cause tears, tantrums or aggression and cause the child to avoid playing that or other games in the future. It may also cause other children to avoid the child. A slight change in schedule, such as having a snack before, rather than after recess, or a seemingly minor unpredictable disappointment (e.g. arriving at the toy store and discovering it is closed) may result in a lengthy and intense upset. Getting a spot of water or dirt on a clean shirt may cause a total emotional breakdown in some children. (see Chapter 8 on sensory sensitivities). Wearing the "wrong" color or not having socks pulled up just right, while perhaps also being a sensory issue, can become a "perfection frustration." Watching children experiencing this kind of reaction, it appears as if the child feels their world has crumbled and he will never be happy again.

Children with anxiety in general often experience this kind of discomfort. Those with PDD and Asperger's disorder seem particularly prone to perfectionist-related distress. Children who have anxiety but are typically developing in other ways, including socially, may spontaneously and naturally engage in play to work through discomfort, to practice coping skills and to arrive at solutions. Children on the autism spectrum tend to *not* use play naturally in this way, so Replays can be particularly effective. By using Replays, the adult can help the child experience the tiniest lack of perfection as tolerable, within what is clearly a pretend arena. By adding playful humor and exaggeration, and then very gradually increasing the degree of variation from perfection, while slowly increasing the realism of the experience, the child becomes increasingly able to tolerate the perceived imperfection. The adult's role is to keep the play feeling fun enough and not upsetting, while gently expanding what the child can tolerate.

Replays with these issues are generally very effective. The play can include figures and props as similar to real life as possible. For schedule-bound children who use a picture schedule in school, dolls can use the actual picture schedule, while the adult playing the "mixed up" teacher can keep changing it around quickly, dropping pieces on the floor, in a way that is clearly funny. As the dolls become increasingly angry and confused, the child can straighten out the schedule and put it in the right order. The teacher can keep asking "Oh you mean THIS FIRST?" moving it all around and mixing it up again. Putting things in a clearly ridiculous order, which the child will recognize as such (FIRST we wash hands, THEN go to the bathroom; first we put JACKETS on then we GO TO BED), helps decrease stress and increase humor. For younger children, visuals and dolls will be needed, while for more verbal or reading children, actual written schedules can be used with a doll or person pretending to become confused and upset.

For children who need to win or be first, Replays can involve many silly games in which being first or winning does not matter to the child. The adult can have two blocks race across the rug with one crying when it loses. The other one can comfort it. Two doll figures or superheroes can similarly race. It is best to begin with a very simple game so it can be played quickly, and the child can briefly and playfully experience the losing. Over time, the child can be encouraged to take one of the blocks, and the adult and child can, in a predictable way, take turns winning. The funnier the losing is, by adding a silly tantrum, the more the child will be drawn to it and will be able to experience the silliness combined with his or her own intuitive negative response to losing.

Relatedly, many children experience perfectionism around creations or other kinds of output. Needing LEGO® or block buildings to appear just right or having drawings look exactly as they are in the child's mind's eye can also cause extreme frustration and agitation. Some children may spend minutes or hours writing and erasing a drawing, number or letter until it looks exactly right and even then may become so frustrated they rip up the paper or otherwise deteriorate behaviorally. Through Replays, the adult can make their own block structure, pretend to become frustrated as the same piece teeters and falls over and over, while the child laughs and fixes it. To address drawing or writing perfectionism, the adult can make their own drawing, "accidentally" scribbling it messily and becoming upset as the child supplies new paper and crayon. The funny part comes as the adult appears to try hard to make it right and there is suspense as to whether it will go right, then humor when "OH NO!!!!" the drawing gets messed up, the block tower falls, or some other accident occurs. The "accident" should be clearly playful enough so the child knows it is "on purpose" within the adult's control. Exaggeration (a big scribble on an otherwise perfectly partially drawn letter, exaggeration of frustration such as laughing while throwing the paper on the floor, etc.) enhances these "signals of play." If one is on the right track, the child will soon join in, making pretend mistakes and laughing.

Many children with anxiety and compulsive tendencies become extremely upset if a toy is slightly broken or a tiny piece is missing, if a crayon breaks, or if a puzzle piece can't be found. An unfamiliar outsider may say "That's no big deal, I'm sure we'll find it/fix it/get another later" and expect the child to calm down. But a familiar insider, such as a parent, will know this is a crisis in the making and will go to great lengths to turn the house upside down to find the missing object, repair the broken item, or find a replacement immediately.

There are many ways to use Replays to approach the issue of broken or missing objects. The adult can make pretend toys by cutting out drawings and turning down a corner or ripping off a tiny edge – whatever the child can tolerate – and pretend to become upset. This may need to be played over and over, especially once the child can tolerate a close approximation of their own experience. The adult can pretend, as the child watches, to hide, cover up or slightly move, again the closest approximation to what the child can tolerate, an object from the child's collection of cars or DVDs and pretend to become upset. The child can find it instantly and make the adult happy. If the child cannot tolerate this with his own toys, the adult can use neutral objects at first, such as a set of spoons or cards or other objects that elicit no emotional reaction, gradually pairing these or giving them properties of the child's objects – e.g. the spoons can develop engines and drive on roads, increasingly approximating the child's beloved cars.

Related obsessive-compulsive issues can make it difficult to get through a typical day. These can include what order clothing is put on in (e.g. child has to have a shirt put on before pants or socks on before the shirt), how food is presented (e.g. sandwich has to be cut into rectangles, not triangles or maybe can't be cut at all; foods cannot be touching on the plate; syrup has to cover every square of waffle). Children may have to leave the house or enter school through a certain door or they feel "off" most of the day. Children may have to touch certain objects (e.g. the sign on the door; the shade on the window) as they enter school or before bed. Sometimes these routines are around somewhat stressful transitions such as going to school or bed, and the routines themselves can decrease stress. However, intervention, including Replays, is recommended when the routines become time-consuming or can't be fulfilled and cause extreme distress for the child when they are not carried out.

As children get older, obsessive-compulsive issues can also evolve into great upset around making mistakes. This can manifest in the child falling apart with sadness or rage and developing great aversions to situations such as being corrected by a teacher or in response to having to rewrite a paragraph or edit a research paper. Being corrected by peers may also elicit severe and negative responses.

Adults can playfully make what, to the child, are very obvious mistakes on a worksheet or homework assignment – obviously adding numbers incorrectly, for example – and the child can gleefully correct them while the adult can pretend to be devastated. Some children cannot tolerate mistakes even within this playful context, so even tinier mistakes are needed such as the adult expressing "Oh no, I made the '5' wrong." For some children the "mistake" has to be invisible initially ("Oh no! I was thinking the answer was '5' but I know it's 6 so I'll write 6."). Sometimes when children verbally object to the adult even playfully giving a wrong answer, the adult can playfully begin to mouth or whisper it, then cover her mouth with a big "OOOPS!" and give the right answer. After doing this several times, usually children can increasingly tolerate the adult saying the "wrong" answer. The key for success is finding the "mistake zone" so the child is able to tolerate some imperfection or variation, giving him or her a sense of control and mastery. Then the goal is to gradually work towards incorporating the nature of the mistake the child actually finds so aversive.

Birthday party fears

Birthday parties, the child's own, or other children's, are a common source of anxiety for many children with PDD, Asperger's and other related issues – so common that we felt they deserved their own section in this book. The combination of the heightened overall excitement that the specialness of the event creates, the loud, busy, unpredictable nature of the crowd, and the unfamiliarity of peers in an often unfamiliar place, in addition to the novel routine, contribute to creating anxiety.

Further, each party includes similar elements, yet each is different. Even if a child becomes comfortable at one birthday party, the next might be completely different and hence recreate the initial anxiety. Singing "Happy Birthday" with clapping, screaming, and candles completely overwhelms many children with anxiety, due to the combination of emotional anticipation and excitement and the unique and intense visual and auditory sensory input. For many children, this birthday party fear can spread to fear of parties, singing or even cakes.

There are several ways to approach birthday parties. Perhaps the simplest way is to begin with "birthday drive-throughs." With this approach, the child picks out a present; parent and child drop it off before the party and leave. A short and sweet birthday visit is better than a long traumatic one. The length of the stay can then be gradually increased. However, the child may miss out on what could become fun. The next stage can include gathering information beforehand, such as the location, agenda, and any surprises, such as a sudden cameo by a clown, then previewing the site and coming for just one "component" of the party (e.g. just the cake or the games) that is most appealing to the child.

Replays are also very effective for birthday party practice. Enlisting the help of peers to add some of the realistic elements, but within a familiar comfortable setting (e.g. at the child's preschool or day care) is very helpful. Adding real props such as party hats, favors and other common props, and some typical party games increases the similarity between the play and the reality. Be sure to make each "play through" different so the child becomes more comfortable with variations on the same general theme. The adult can exaggerate fear of singing ("OH NO, NOT that SILLY BIRTHDAY SONG!!!"), or the games ("I HOPE we don't have to play that BLINDFOLD game – I HATE having my eyes covered"), and playfully encourage the child to participate as you protest, using lines or behaviors from the child's repertoire but gradually showing enjoyment.

Group practice of the actual singing with the adult and even a few children, engaging in "whisper-singing" "Happy Birthday" with "whisper-claps" at the end, can help in desensitizing the anxious child who has particular upset around the song. He or she can then be encouraged to gradually turn up the volume and gain control by using a "thumbs up or thumbs down" signal, so as to be in charge of the adult or the peer group.

Other fears or phobias

While many fears and phobias are discussed in Chapter 8, other non-sensory-based fears or phobias can also be effectively treated with Replays. Some children develop fears around events that evoke strong emotions, such as scary parts in videos or books. Children with such fears may demand that a particular page be skipped or that a video be "fast-forwarded." Sometimes, these fears pass once a child has seen the movie or read the book a few times. What once was an object of fear can become a new passion, much as typically developing children and adults love to watch the same scary movie over and over. However, for very anxious children, this can evolve into fears of many videos or TV shows and can spread to figures related to these shows, peer play related to these movies or shows, and even to fear of TV in general or going to movies. When this problem is "spreading" rather than improving, Replays can be very useful.

Depending on the child's level of pretend, play acting through the scary part, with silly very different figures (e.g. dinosaurs in a movie about witches) but enough similarity so the child recognizes the similarity, can be effective. Switching roles – in other words, having the adult pretend to be extremely scared and need to hold the child's hand while the child reassures the adult, is a useful tactic. If the child can't tolerate direct play of the story or movie plot, initial pretend play may have to be more distant in plot but only involve some overlapping characteristics. For example, a child afraid of clowns may need to first play through putting stickers, then "face paint" on plastic figures, gradually approaching clown-like figures.

Replays for fear of masks are often very effective, as they can be, over time, played out fully realistically. Begin by using very obvious, immediately removable masks, even a plain sheet of paper with holes cut for eyes can be used. The adult can put the paper "mask" over a doll and pretend to be afraid. Typically, the child will pull it off quickly and reassure the scared adult. This can be varied by having the child wear the paper, a figure or doll wear the paper, and then increasingly approximating real party masks on familiar dolls. Face paint or face crayons can then be used in very small amounts on dolls with the adult pretending to be afraid.

Many children are afraid of remote-operated toys, or toys that can be activated to do something realistic (e.g. toy dogs that can walk; cars that run on their own; dolls that talk). These fears may be caused by the emotional confusion created regarding exactly what is real and what is not. Fear of remote or self-moving toys can decrease through Replays by having the adult pretend to operate a toy that clearly doesn't move such as a block or cloth or plastic doll. The child sees the adult pretend to make it jump and the adult then pretends to be scared. Over time, the adult can hand the toy to the child who will hopefully pretend to make it operate and the adult can pretend to be scared. Role-switching and toy-shifting helps the child to generalize. Gradually, real remote or moving toys can be used. It is important to have the child observe the batteries being removed (with the batteries removed as viewed by the child, they know that the toy will not move unexpectedly). Once the child can playfully activate these toys, the batteries can be put in and the adult can give the child warning ("1, 2, 3…" or "Ready, set…"). When the child says or signals "Go" the adult can operate the toy for a second or two. The child can continue to be in control and will likely enjoy the play this way, as the unpredictability factor is no longer present. The movement can be extended in time as the child's tolerance increases. The child can hold or operate the toy with the adult pretending to be scared. This may not always help with new toys but will usually be sufficient to desensitize the child to toys that may belong to a sibling or be part of a classroom. It may also reduce the child's discomfort with new toys.

It is important to note that Replays are one of many ways of helping children with significant anxiety and compulsive issues. A predictable and comfortable environment, building in happy, fun times and increasing physical activity can all reduce anxiety.

Anxiety sometimes runs in families. If parents are aware that they too are anxious, working to decrease their anxiety can greatly help their child as well, because children with and without PDD are often very sensitive to anxiety in loved ones. Other approaches include child yoga, guided visualization, sensory integration approaches, biofeedback, as well as medication. Replays can be used in conjunction with any of these other techniques.

PART IV

Adaptive Replays across Different Settings

10

Replays with Siblings and Peers

The human race has only one really effective weapon and that is laughter.

— Mark Twain

All siblings have complex relationships. They love each other, despise each other, defend, resent, are drawn to and avoid each other. Sometimes, they are unbearably jealous of each other; other times, they are loving and fiercely protective. For most people, the relationship with a sibling is the longest relationship they will ever have.

Hard to find help

There is an increasing number of articles and books written for parents that provide helpful tips and suggestions for improving sibling relationships. *Siblings Without Rivalry* by Adele Faber and Elaine Mazlish, one of the first popular "how to" books on the subject, has some excellent strategies and approaches for tackling sibling spats. Others include T. Berry Brazelton and J.D. Sparrow's *Understanding Sibling Rivalry* and *The Baffled Parent's Guide to Sibling Rivalry* by Marian Edelman Borden. These books focus primarily on typically developing children and the interventions and strategies described require age-appropriate or close-to age-appropriate speech, language processing, and cognitive function.

Books that discuss children with disabilities and sibling issues, such as *Brothers and Sisters of Disabled Children* by Peter Burke, and *The Experiences and Views of Disabled Children and their Siblings* by Claire Connors and Kristen Stalker focus on helping the typically developing child understand and cope with a brother or sister who has a disability. While this literature is invaluable to families and validating for the typically developing child, there is little written about approaches that help the child with the disability cope with her own behavior, thereby improving interactions with a sibling or parents.

In families in which a child has autism or related communication or social problems, especially when the children are young and close in age, misunderstandings and conflicts arise among siblings, just as in any other family, and, depending on the children and family, it is likely that they occur more frequently and perhaps with greater intensity. Sometimes, the causes of conflict are not obvious and may remain unknown, and the solutions may not only be different from what one might expect but also require creative approaches and multiple attempts.

Often parents and older or typically developing siblings just want the interfering behavior to stop and don't have the time or luxury of sitting back, reflecting on the causes and systematically coming up with a plan to eliminate the behavior permanently. The result is an endless cycle of negative behavior, increasing anger, more disruption and then leaving the "scene of the crime." The underlying cause and emotions associated with the original upset are never addressed.

Managing conflicting and confusing emotions

While sometimes children get along well and conflict can even be less than with only typically developing children, perhaps because the children are not competing as much for the same sorts of needs, it is not uncommon for families with a child with autism to experience a unique set of stressors. Learning how to contribute to family functioning and establishing cooperative, reciprocal relationships with family members, including siblings, often takes much longer for families including a child with autism. A child who sees her brother "get away with" not doing chores or misbehaving in public or perhaps getting rewarded and praised for the simplest accomplishments may, understandably, become angry, resentful or embarrassed. At the same time, she may feel she has to defend her brother against others who may tease or reject him. Conversely, a child with autism may become sad when she sees her younger sister surpass her in reading and math, play field hockey and socialize with friends, while she can't begin to understand the complex rules of reading, sports or social interactions.

Sibling relationships may result in frequent arguments and misunderstandings, tension, or worse, in total family chaos and unresolved anger among all family members. While feeling conflicted or ambivalent, it is not uncommon for parents of children with and without disabilities to take sides, with one protecting the child who doesn't know any better or has fewer coping mechanisms, and the other defending and empathizing with the typical child whose life often seems disrupted or restricted because of a sibling who can't learn how to "act normal." Some families take a "divide and conquer" approach in order to keep the peace: Dad goes off in one direction with the typically developing children, while Mom manages the child with social and behavioral problems in another environment. As one mother put it, "I feel like we are two single-parent families living under the same roof."

Clearly for single parents, there are a unique set of challenges, trying simultaneously to meet the needs of children who may actually have quite opposite needs (e.g. one needs to get out and do things; the other does best at home; one needs friends; the other cannot tolerate crowds, etc.). Further, it can be more challenging to find friends or others who are comfortable babysitting the child with special needs.

Can Replays help? The answer is "Sometimes"

Take, for example, the Burns family. William, age 8, has an undiagnosed developmental disability with some autistic features. His language was delayed and, although he now talks, his speech is halting and limited to asking for food, a particular toy or talking obsessively about preferred topics, such as types of airplanes and models of cars. He often becomes anxious and perseverative, which prevents him from appropriately interacting with both adults and peers. At times, he is able to interact with classmates at school with support from his teacher and a one-to-one assistant, but he doesn't play with friends outside school or participate in after-school activities. Staffing is limited and students are expected to be more independent than William is for these programs, his parents have been told. So he spends most of his after-school hours and weekends at home, "bothering me and looking for trouble," according to his sister.

Polar opposites

William's six-year-old sister, Alice, who is extroverted, takes ballet and swimming lessons, loves to perform and plays frequently with neighborhood children. She hosts pretend tea parties for her friends and their dolls, decorates the walls and windows with her artwork and plays dress-up. Recently, she danced in her first recital.

While William doesn't want to play with the girls or engage in the same activities, he does realize at some level that he is "different," and not as socially capable. As a result, in part, he has become increasingly hostile and aggressive toward Alice, hitting, kicking, and screaming at her whenever she tries to play with him. He also interferes when she is with her friends.

On a few occasions, their parents tried to include both children in family outings, which ended in disaster. Once, when the four of them went out for ice cream, William crawled up on the table and pushed Alice's ice cream into her lap, complete with fudge sauce and whipped cream. She began to cry and hit William, at which point Mrs. Burns scolded her. William put his hands over his ears and began to scream. Mr. Burns quickly paid and rushed the family out the door and into the car. Nobody had ice cream that night, and everyone ended up angry and resentful, not knowing how to prevent the same thing from happening again.

On another occasion, the family attended a musical performance geared to young children. It seemed to be going well until, during intermission, the Burns ran into one of Alice's friends and her family. When the girls greeted each other enthusiastically, diverting Alice's attention, William began to scream loudly, "Alice is stupid! Alice is stupid!" This continued during the entire intermission, despite his parents' efforts to calm him. Then William refused to go back into the theatre for the second half of the concert. Alice had an emotional outburst, too, screaming "I hate him! He ruins everything!"

Enter the therapist, who first met with Mr. and Mrs. Burns alone in their home. While she told them she could work with each child individually and then together, she advised them to additionally find another therapist for Alice, someone with whom she could connect, talk, play, and complain – someone she didn't have to share with William. She would work with William, however. The therapist noticed a large dollhouse, furniture and figures of mom, dad, several children and pets to play with in their playroom, in addition to the usual cars, trucks, and blocks. The first time she met William, she took out the dollhouse and evaluated his ability to play symbolically:

"Here comes Dad," she said. "Oh William… It's time for dinner," she called, making the toy Dad yell from the kitchen window. "William, dinner!" she repeated.

William responded, "No! I hate dinner." He ran to the other side of the room. She took the boy figure and went after him, placing the toy in his hand, repeating, "No, no, no! I hate dinner." William repeated "Hate dinner, hate dinner, hate dinner." With hand-over-hand facilitation, she made the boy figure jump up and down and mimic William.

"Hate dinner!" He pulled his hand away from hers, continuing to yell and making the boy jump up and down. "Hate dinner! Hate dinner!" he continued.

The therapist realized that, while William's pretend play skills were just emerging, he did have some symbolic understanding and that Replays would probably work for him. At the very least, his pretend play skills would be enhanced through the repetitive acting out of familiar emotional encounters.

Laughter: the best indication that it's working

During the next session, the therapist set up the dollhouse family at a table. She made the toy Dad say, "Let's all have ice cream," and, with exaggerated affect, said, "Ummmm!" William repeated "Ice cream.

Ummmm." She repeated this sequence with the toy family, and asked William, "What is the mom (dad, sister, dog) saying?" and he repeated, "Ice cream. Ummmm" each time. Then she put toy bowls in front of each figure, including the dog, which William thought especially funny. He repeated several more times, "Ice cream. Ummmm." And he laughed.

During this drama, William's eye contact increased and his affect was appropriate, if somewhat exaggerated. He and the therapist laughed together and connected emotionally. She added several elements to increase the silliness, for example, making the dog say, "Ice cream. Ummmm. Arf! Arf!," which William thought was hysterical.

But then the therapist "dumped" the ice cream in the sister doll's lap and made her cry, "Whaaa. Whaaa. Don't do that. Whaaa."

William laughed and immediately joined in, repeating the same scenario several times, including dumping the ice cream and making the sister doll cry. But his laughter then turned to tears – real tears of sadness, and he stopped playing.

The therapist made the sister doll say, "Don't worry, William. I know you didn't mean it. Let's eat our ice cream." And then she made the toy girl (sister) kiss the toy William, then the real William. But he was inconsolable.

Not anticipating this reaction, the therapist thought quickly and made the boy (who represented William) say, "I'm sorry. I didn't want to hurt you. Let me help clean that up. Let's have fun and eat our ice cream." She waited to see what William would do – what he could understand and if he would "catch on."

Although William seemed confused, he stopped crying and began playing with both the toy boy and girl again, making them pretend to eat their ice cream. While William didn't "get" *all* the subtleties of the Replay, at least not on the first or even fifth attempt, he did feel the emotional impact and was able to recover and return to the play. Interestingly, when the therapist arrived for the next session, William greeted her and said, "Play ice cream?"

Several sessions later, after replaying the ice cream scenario, the therapist suggested making a book together, similar to a Social Story™

but, rather than providing instructions, it included, along with very basic stick figures and conversation "bubbles," the following story:

Title: The Ice Cream Story

Page 1. One day William, Alice, Mommy, and Daddy went out for ice cream.

Page 2. The ice cream arrived and everyone was happy.

Page 3. Then William got angry. He didn't know why.

Page 4. William climbed on the table and dumped Alice's ice cream all over her. Alice began to cry.

Page 5. Mommy got angry and yelled. Then Daddy got angry and yelled.

Page 6. The whole family left and didn't eat their ice cream.

William enjoyed making the book and pretended to cry every time they got to Page 4. Sometimes he cried real tears. The therapist then suggested writing an alternative ending. Pages 1–3 remained the same. Then the story changed:

Page 4. Although he was angry, William sat quietly and waited for his ice cream. He told himself, "I feel angry, but I won't do anything upsetting. I'll eat my ice cream."

Page 5. Everyone ate their ice cream and said, "Hooray! Ice cream!"

Page 6. The whole family ate their ice cream together. William let Alice taste some of his, and Alice let William taste some of hers.

Add a happy ending

After writing the alternative ending, the therapist and William played it through several times, sometimes adding other humorous touches, like having the dog saying "Yuck! I don't like strawberry," or making Alice say, "I'm going to give all my ice cream to William." The therapist had been sharing the Replays with William's parents all along, encouraging them to attempt another outing eventually.

After feeling like the story was well stored in William's cerebral "play center," the therapist gave William's parents both versions of the story and instructed them to go out again for ice cream. She made an extra copy for his sister. First, they all read Version 1, calling it *The Ice Cream Story: The Old Days*. They also read Version 2, *The Ice Cream Story: The New Days*. Alice especially liked the part about sharing different flavors.

The family then acted it out, with Alice joining in, patiently and increasingly playfully playing her part.

Replays is generally most effective when the actual siblings can join in the play. This requires that the sibling is old enough to understand the pretend aspect, and also has enough tolerance to play through the scene the "wrong" way. If the sibling is not ready, pre-teaching, as in this situation, where Alice was initially too sensitive about the issue to participate, is a useful place to start. Once the child on the autism spectrum has mastered the pretend, the sibling can watch the child and adult play and gradually join in.

It actually worked the first time! The Burns family was able to get through an ice cream outing with only a spilled glass of water and a complaint about the size of the chocolate chips, but no screaming or tears. Now they regularly go out for ice cream on Friday nights and have begun to address some of William's other difficulties, especially his disruptive behaviors when Alice's friends are at the house, through Replays.

Replays worked for William for several reasons:

1. He had sufficient language and pretend play capacity to be able to understand and participate in different versions of the play.

2. He could identify some emotions in himself and in others.

Had William not been able to identify his feelings as anger or sadness, he may have gotten confused or he may not have been able to control his impulse to climb on the table and dump the ice cream. Since he played it over so many times using the dollhouse figures, he knew what was going to happen next and could anticipate the arrival of the ice cream and the dissipation of his angry feelings.

Although not every sibling conflict lends itself to a Replays solution, family members and therapists can often use creative play, numerous repetitions, story telling and alternative endings to, literally, change the future.

Snatching and grabbing toys

Replays can be very helpful for this problem. Toy grabbing is a common problem among siblings and children in general. Typically developing children usually eventually learn not to do it as a result of parent and sibling reactions and perhaps a few reminders. However, sometimes siblings, particularly when they are young, close in age, and one or more have social, communication, anxiety and/or sensory challenges, persist in this, far beyond the age when it may be tolerated.

Sometimes parents of twins or children close in age will buy two of a toy hoping to avoid this; however, even this often does not help as they each want the *other* child's toy or one child wants both. There are several reasons why this is so common. First, toys in use are virtually always more appealing than toys lying on the shelf or floor. A toy car being pushed across a pretend highway in the seam of the sofa, complete with sound effects by one's brother can suddenly make it necessary to have it right away – although it held no interest a few minutes before, when it was lying upside down in a toy pile. Second, jealousy that may arise about almost anything (and usually elicits parent attention) can exacerbate a sibling's desire to have what the other one has.

Replays targeting toy grabbing are fun to do and children usually enjoy and respond well to them. The adult can have two figures (dolls, animals) pull on the same toy which can be anything disposable and that can rip (e.g. a tissue; a cut-out picture of a toy; two pop beads) until it breaks in half using the language or sounds the children use. Keep the language simple and the props more realistic for young or less verbal children ("MINE! NO MINE! NO MINE!"). Two adults acting this out is typically VERY amusing for young children, especially if they over-dramatize the action, and one falls down as the other one pulls the toy away. As in other Replays, eventually the figures or actual people decide to take turns, the children increasingly take roles, and then the adult can draw a multi-picture story.

Getting a big reaction

Siblings know each other unbelievably well, including knowing just what will set off a big reaction in their brother or sister. Children prone to "big reactions" such as children with significant regulatory, sensory, and anxiety issues, are prime targets for siblings. A teenager, who is usually very helpful and patient with her 11-year-old brother with Asperger's syndrome and anxiety, knows he becomes completely unglued if his LEGO® structures are moved. Occasionally, if she has had a bad day and he is getting on her nerves, she may go over and snatch a tiny LEGO® piece from one of his numerous structures that colonize the house and elicit questions and puzzling looks from her friends. Predictably, this sets off her brother's shrieking which may also get him in trouble. A five-year-old girl knows from experience that, if her seven-year-old brother with Asperger's syndrome, anxiety, and sensory issues just hears the words "Bees everywhere" whispered, he will begin screaming uncontrollably; she experiments and learn that even hearing the word "bees" upsets him. While they usually get along well, they have moments, as all siblings do, when they get angry with each other, and the girl may use one of her "secret weapons" to create mayhem in the family.

For such issues, direct Replays with the child with anxiety or autism can of course be beneficial. However, doll play with figures representing both children can offer great comic relief and help both children, when this is possible, "act out" angry scenes, thus replacing the real thing. Interestingly, within doll play, the child with anxiety and sensory issues can often tolerate what she can't in real life, such as having a doll say "Bees everywhere" in a predictable fashion, as opposed to having her sister say it without warning and with malicious intent.

First, this can be done as a performance by a parent or both parents together. They can manipulate figures or act out the scene, depending on what the children respond best to, and the children can gradually become more involved. It is important not to step over the line – that is, parents should not appear to be teasing or making fun of the child who has the big reaction; by signaling that this is JUST PLAY by smiling or adding silly variations on the scenario, such interpretations can be avoided but be silly enough to get the children laughing and, ultimately, cooperating.

References

Borden, M.E. (2003) *The Baffled Parent's Guide to Sibling Rivalry*. New York: McGraw Hill.

Brazelton, T.B. and Sparrow, J.D. (2005) *Understanding Sibling Rivalry: The Brazelton Way*. Cambridge, MA: Da Capa Press.

Burke, P. (2003) *Brothers and Sisters of Disabled Children*. London: Jessica Kingsley Publishers.

Connors, C. and Stalker, K. (2003) *The Experiences and Views of Disabled Children and their Siblings*. London: Jessica Kingsley Publishers.

Faber, A. and Mazlish, E. (1987) *Siblings Without Rivalry*. New York: W.W. Norton and Co.

11

Implementing Replays in Educational Settings

> Whatever you can do or dream you can begin it. Boldness has genius, power and magic in it. Begin it now.
>
> — *Johann Wolfgang von Goethe*

Early childhood classroom – an ideal setting for Replays

The classroom is an environment in which doing Replays can be helpful to teachers and students alike. Preschool and kindergarten particularly lend themselves to approaching problems, such as separation anxiety, arguments between students, hurt feelings and competition over who will be the first to give the correct answer, be the special helper, or lead the line to the playground, through play and specifically Replays. Situations occur in which conflicts arise many times each day. In fact, it is the job of the early childhood educator to teach students how to get along, and it is in such classrooms that children learn to approach conflict, learn coping skills, tolerate and even appreciate different ideas and perspectives, and come up with solutions.

This is an era in which inclusion is the trend – and a growing one – that is, children with and without physical, learning, and social or emotional problems are being educated in the same classrooms, at least for part of the day. Not surprisingly, behavioral difficulties, individual problems, and misunderstandings between students arise, just as they do in any classroom. The difference is that these problems may have different underlying causes and more complex solutions for those with identified disabilities. A teacher who can rely on rational discussions, at least to some extent, with a typically developing student about what went wrong, and strategize about how to do it better the next time, may not have the same success with a student for whom spoken language is more difficult to process, one who learns at a slower pace and/or in different ways from typically developing peers or one whose emotions interfere with internalizing new strategies and solutions. In such cases, Replays, sometimes coupled with other relational approaches or behavioral interventions, can be more successful than relying on spoken language and reason.

Take for example, the following chronic problem which occurred at preschool.

The Circle Time fiasco

Roger, a delightful and energetic four-year-old with a diagnosis of high-functioning autism spectrum disorder, was placed in an integrated preschool classroom. Roger was verbal, able to interact with peers during physical games on the playground and sometimes, with support, during short, small group activities in the classroom. So it was thought that he would thrive among typically developing preschoolers, whom he could imitate and learn from. Roger, however, was quite impulsive and quick to react. He would frequently hit, yell or simply take a toy that he wanted to play with, whether it was on the shelf or in someone else's hands. He often missed the non-verbal cues that his classmates had come to understand: a stern glance from the teacher, nodding or shaking her head, or holding a finger up to her lips to signal silence. So Roger didn't respond to limits because he didn't understand the limits; he did what he wanted, when he wanted.

At first, Roger's classmates were attracted to his energy and what they perceived as funny and mischievous antics. This is often the case; children who sometimes have the same desire to yell out, hit or kick a peer, but who have more impulse control and are able to inhibit feelings, enjoy watching someone else do it. They may even encourage "bad"

"Circle Time"

behavior. But Roger's classmates soon grew weary of his control over the classroom. All activity would come to a screeching halt because Roger snatched toys, screamed if he didn't get his way and even pushed and hit his peers during Circle Time. They began to avoid him and, as he stopped getting the attention that was partially driving him, his behaviors escalated.

Many of Roger's peers went home with horror stories about school, sometimes embellishing them as is typical for preschoolers, and some children began to act out in class as well as at home. The teachers found the situation untenable. Parents, too, began to point to Roger when anything went wrong; if a child had a tantrum at home or hit a younger sibling, they assumed he was imitating Roger. One parent even demanded that Roger be "expelled from school." So, rather than providing an appropriate and mutually beneficial inclusive environment for all students, Roger was scapegoated. His parents were disheartened. They even considered placing him in a class for behaviorally challenged children as the teachers, students, and other parents became increasingly unhappy and anxious. As one teacher put it, "I dread coming to work; my students aren't happy; I'm not happy; and nobody is learning anything."

After several meetings with staff, parents, and a number of outside consultants, the teacher assigned a one-to-one aide to Roger in order to keep his behavior "in check." For a couple of weeks, this seemed to be working. When Roger hit, yelled or acted out at Circle Time, his aide would remove him and sit with him in the far corner of the room. But over time, rather than decreasing his negative behaviors, they began to escalate and disruptions became even more frequent. Roger rapidly learned that if he hit, pushed or screamed, he would be "rewarded" with removal from Circle Time and more one-to-one attention. He didn't have to participate with the rest of the class and could get his aide's undivided attention. She and the teacher then tried ignoring Roger's behaviors, but it was impossible; he was too disruptive and hurtful to other students.

Although Roger had some major communication and social difficulties, his play was becoming more symbolic. He talked on a toy telephone, put toy figures and animals in a school bus, pushed it down ramps that he built, with assistance, in the block corner and especially enjoyed crashing cars into each other. So his teacher and aide planned an intervention using Replays to teach him better behaviors. They decided to start with Circle Time, as it was a critical period of the day, occurring early in the morning, and it often set the tone for the rest of the day. If Roger behaved during Circle Time, which he occasionally did, the remainder of the day went relatively smoothly. When Roger was disruptive, staff and students became more anxious and agitated during the day, waiting for "the next shoe to drop."

Mondays were the hardest for Roger, as they are for many children and adults. He had difficulty transitioning after a weekend at home where there was much less structure. As an only child, he didn't have a lot of competition and his needs could be met almost immediately. At a particular Monday morning Circle, Roger began screaming almost immediately because it was not his turn to be "the Weatherman" that day: "My turn! My turn," he yelled and reached out to push a classmate aside. In an effort to minimize the chaos, Roger's aide swung into action. But, rather than simply removing him to the back of the classroom and doing a puzzle or playing with a shape sorter, Roger's aide took him aside and announced "We can't miss Circle Time, so we are going to do it over here," and she gathered up three stuffed animals – a beaver, a dog, and a pig – and arranged them in a semi-circle around Roger. At first he was bewildered, but looked on with interest.

The aide then began to go through a typical Circle Time routine: "Now Piglet, you are the Weatherman today. Doggie, you can be Weatherman tomorrow, and Beaver, you have to wait until Wednesday." She moved Piglet to the front of the circle, but then "made" Beaver yell, "No! No! I want to be Weatherman! It's my turn! You sit down." And she made Beaver hit Piglet. When Piglet started to cry, Doggie intervened, saying, "Beaver, don't hurt Piglet. I know it's hard to wait your turn, but we ALL have to wait. Look how sad he is." And Doggie gave Piglet a hug.

Roger continued to watch with surprise and intrigue. He had never seen these familiar animals "cry" or express any emotion. As the aide carried on, replaying the scene several times with exaggerated affect, he became more engaged. At one point, the aide had Doggie ask Roger if he wanted to give Piglet a hug so "he won't be sad," and Roger grabbed him and held him tightly.

This was the first sign that Roger was catching on or, at the very least, developing some empathy for Piglet, who had been yelled at and hit by impatient, impulsive Beaver. When Circle Time ended for both the students and animals, Roger returned to small group activities, during which he was more successful, and to his one-to-one therapy sessions. However, he continued to have a few yelling episodes and grabbed toys from peers.

The next morning, Roger's aide asked him, "Do you want to have Circle Time with the class or with the animals?" He gazed at the back of the room and the animal corner. So they proceeded to set up Circle Time as they had the day before. Again, the aide played out the scene as she had the previous day, but this time she made Doggie the Weatherman. And again Beaver yelled "No! No!! I'm the Weatherman. It's my turn!" And Beaver hit Doggie this time. She repeated this scenario over and over until Roger grabbed Doggie and gave him a hug. Roger also grabbed and hugged Piglet.

It was not entirely clear if he was "getting it," and understanding that Beaver, like Roger, had a tough time taking turns and was aggressive with other animals and sometimes pushed his friends. But Roger did clearly enjoy comforting the animals after they were hurt, so the aide decided to capitalize on his emotional reaction and desire to make them feel better. She then altered the routine slightly:

"Roger, I don't know what to do about Beaver. He keeps hitting and trying to be the Weatherman when it isn't his turn. He's really mean to his friends. What should I do?" First Roger said, "Hit," grabbed Beaver and started to hit him. The aide, without judgment or a scolding tone of voice, replied, "Hmmm...I don't think that will work. Maybe you should *show* him how to be good at Circle Time." Roger reacted almost immediately and screamed, "Beaver, sit." and his aide said in a very animated manner, "Outstanding idea! Beaver, sit. Roger, sit. Beaver, you can be Weatherman tomorrow!" The other animals chimed in, "Good job, Beaver. You are a good friend."

Roger's aide shared this play routine with his parents, recommending that they try it at home before dinner or at bedtime, and she sent all three animals home with him. Although his parents reported that he became more aggressive with the animals (Beaver really hit hard!) than they would have liked, they reported that Roger seemed genuinely concerned and wanted to comfort them. They were pleased, as he had rarely shown this kind of empathy or relatedness in his play with stuffed animals prior to this.

The next day at school, the aide suggested that Roger bring Beaver to Circle Time to see if he could sit and wait his turn. But, she added, "It could be really hard. He's going to need a lot of help." She began by commanding, "Beaver, sit!" and Roger repeated, "Beaver, sit!" The teacher, who had been checking in with the aide several times a day, asked the rest of the class to help, too: "Let's all help Beaver sit," and the class replied in unison, "Beaver, sit!" The routine continued for several more days and into the next week, with children saying "Beaver, sit," to Roger at various times of day in an effort to connect with him. Roger seemed so wrapped up in Beaver's ability to sit that his own difficulties, at least during Circle Time, diminished. And, when it was his turn to be

Weatherman, Beaver went along with him, with prompting, funny comments and kudos from both his teachers and classmates.

On subsequent occasions, when Roger became restless or started to yell or get pushy at Circle Time, his aide would make one of the animals – either Beaver, Doggie, or another animal, yell, "My turn! You sit down," and then tell Roger, "Oh-oh…I think Doggie needs your help. What should we tell him?" Roger and often his classmates would reply, "Doggie (or Beaver or Piglet) sit!" and that was usually enough to get Roger to stop yelling, cooperate, and focus.

This use of Replays in integrated classrooms benefits not only the child with special needs but also the typical peers, who tend to develop more of an understanding of what makes the child "tick," and hence why different people can respond to the same situation so differently. Roger is no longer viewed as "naughty" but as trying to express his needs and needing other ways to do this. Further, the typical peers also develop an increased repertoire of ways to play with each other as well as with the child with special needs.

Replays were successful in this situation for several reasons: Roger was bright and quick to catch on; he had some rudimentary pretend play skills; he had some language; and he had a supportive and collaborative school team that truly wanted to fix the problem rather than placing him in a behavioral class in which negative and disruptive behaviors would be the norm, rather than the exception.

Unintended consequences

In follow-up conversations with Roger's teachers, it became apparent that the Replays continued to work in some but not all situations. And, sometimes, Roger used them inappropriately. For example, although Roger had fewer aggressive or disruptive incidents, he would "blame" Beaver when he did do something wrong. Beaver, and not Roger, spit water from the water fountain at a classmate. Piglet, and not Roger, ruined the block castle that three children had worked on for days. In such cases, Roger's teachers told him that they noticed that "You participated too, so you have a "time out" along with Beaver, and then you must apologize too."

Replays in the self-contained classroom

Although they may take a different form, teachers and therapists can also use Replays in self-contained or homogeneous classrooms in which all students have similar communication, social/emotional or behavioral needs. Of course, the Replays need to be tailored to the developmental level of the student(s) and have to be made accessible through simplified words and actions, many more repetitions and perhaps a slower pace. Replays may also work better for children who are more challenged in one or more areas if they are implemented outdoors or in a gym or other playspace in which running, chasing, and other large motor activities can occur. Increasing action and minimizing speech and language may yield more positive results in such programs (see Chapter 6 about tailoring Replays for active children with short attention spans).

It is important for the teacher and other classroom staff to design the classroom environment so that Replays can be implemented easily and sometimes spontaneously. This means having a variety of toy figures on hand, such as animals, puppets, action figures (Spider-Man®, Wonder Woman®) and especially figures based on current and popular children's television programs and videos. Although teachers and parents may feel that commercial products are less desirable than some of the more appealing (at least to adults) and attractive toys available, children are more likely to recognize, identify with, and be motivated by TV and video characters. A variety of toy cars, trucks, airplanes and other vehicles, and a dollhouse, garage or car wash and other play sets will also come in handy.

"Instant Replays" can be used frequently around small recurrent issues in a variety of settings including structured teaching settings of all children with special needs such as Applied Behavioral Analysis (ABA) classes for children with autism. For example, for a child who regularly doesn't want to sit down for "work time" the teacher can have Elmo refuse to sit down for work, get up, have the teacher tell him to sit back down, etc. in a playful fashion over and over, increasingly engaging the child. Eventually, Elmo sits down in the chair next to the child. Typically the child will soon sit down and continue to have Elmo "act out." A child distracted from a table-top task or teacher-directed task, by a bug bite or bandaid can readily be redirected to instant quick Replays where a doll has a bandaid or bug bite and keeps scratching it while the teacher, and soon the child, tells the doll "No!" playfully.

Replays were used successfully in a small, highly structured class-room for children on the autism spectrum, in which there were four students, one lead teacher and two paraprofessionals. Since the adult:student ratio was high, specific problems could be addressed in a timely manner. Rather than trying to maintain order, which may be the immediate goal in a larger, less structured and supervised setting, the teacher or aide could intervene immediately, teaching new skills not only to the child who was having difficulty but to the rest of the class as well.

Wendy, a seven-year-old girl with a diagnosis of PDD–NOS and major mood swings, enjoyed playing at the playground near her urban school setting. She and her classmates went there nearly every day, as long as the weather permitted. She loved the slide, swings, and colorful climbing frame. Her teacher noted that she was the most animated and socially connected when she was outdoors, running around and playing on the equipment. But she didn't especially enjoy the long walk there and back, which, under the best circumstances, took ten minutes in each direction.

Wendy was considerably smaller than her classmates, all boys, and fatigued easily. Most days, Wendy would start out well and walk with the group. But several times a week she would, without warning, "flop" down on the ground and refuse to go any further. Sometimes, she would just sit curled up on the ground, silent and inert; other times she would cry or scream, "Far away, far away." Her teacher, wanting to make the most of the time the class had outside, would simply pick her up and encourage her to walk, which was most often unsuccessful and would result in other children becoming agitated and restless. When she was really desperate, she would pick Wendy up and carry her. While this got the job done – in other words, the group got to the playground and had time to run around, swing, and slide – Wendy was not learning how to cope. Worse, she was learning that, even if she did flop on the ground, it didn't matter because someone would carry her anyway.

The teacher tried a variety of approaches at the suggestion of the school psychologist. "Time outs" didn't work, as Wendy would scream for the entire time at the playground, her classmates got upset, and her flopping didn't decrease. Keeping her back at the classroom and denying her playground time was worse: she didn't get the benefit of physical play and she had fewer opportunities to learn appropriate behaviors because she didn't understand the connection between her flopping on the ground and staying in the classroom.

Reluctantly, the teacher agreed to try Replays. Although in theory she liked the idea of replaying the problematic event, she was skeptical about Wendy's ability to understand and make the connection.

She decided to use a red Teletubby, because it was one of Wendy's favorite toys; it was even more appropriate because Teletubbies have short legs, often take walks together outside, fall down, bump into things, and are largely non-verbal. First, she replayed the flopping down scene in the classroom, using all four Teletubbies. The red one (Po) always flopped down, and the others, using high-pitched voices and limited language, said "Stand up, Stand up," and "Let's go. Let's go."

Wendy and her classmates enjoyed the drama because they all were familiar with Teletubbies.

However, during the next walk to the playground, Wendy, again, flopped down and refused to move. The teacher did the same Replay the next day, with the same result: although the children loved the Teletubbies, it seemed to have no effect on Wendy's behavior.

The following day, the teacher played a Teletubbies CD, which she had borrowed, before, and as a background to, the same Replay. All the students recognized the music immediately and were even more enthusiastic and attentive than previously. On the walk to the playground that day, the teacher played the music on a portable CD player. Wendy was attentive to the music and didn't flop down at all. Back at the classroom, she wanted to play with the Teletubby for the better part of the afternoon and pointed to the CD player several times. She also tossed the Teletubby around on the floor.

The next day, the teacher took both the CD player and the Teletubby to the playground, and Wendy seemed to be doing well. But only yards from the playground Wendy again flopped on the ground. With the music still playing, the teacher made the Teletubby flop down right next to Wendy, saying "Too far. Too Far. Tired. Tired." She and the aides cued the other three students to say, "Stand up. Let's go," which they did, repeatedly. After several minutes, Wendy joined in, rousing the Teletubby from his lying-down position and chanting, "Let's go. Let's go. Let's go."

Wendy began taking the Teletubby to the playground every day. At first, she would flop down, throw the Teletubby down and command him to "Stand up," or say "Let's go." Sometimes the teacher would play the CD; other times, she would sing or hum the Teletubbies' song. Over time, however, Wendy began walking to the playground without flopping – and without bringing the Teletubby.

Although every behavioral problem isn't as easy to solve, this one demonstrates the necessity of manipulating different components until something "clicks." In this case, the addition of the music seemed to help Wendy regulate and make an important connection. Because it was upbeat, cheerful and familiar to the whole group of students, they responded positively and appropriately. By playing the music *and* taking the Teletubby on the walk to the playground, Wendy was more able to enjoy the music and rhythm of the walk, become part of the action, and participate in the solution to her problem.

12

Replays and Technology

For the wise man looks into space and he knows there is no
limited dimension.

— Lao-Tsu

Like it or not, technology has become deeply embedded into play at
every age and developmental stage. That's not necessarily bad news,
and some would argue that it's advantageous to have the skills needed to
move characters around on a screen, manipulate virtual environments,
and search for hidden clues and treasures. While nobody would deny
that many computer and video games have aggressive and violent components, an increasing number do tap into cognitive, especially
problem-solving skills, fine motor abilities and hand–eye coordination.
Some are truly educational, clever, and fun.

The purpose of this chapter is not to convince the reader of the evils
of gaming nor its benefits, but rather to show how to use electronic
gaming and other technologies in combination with Replays to solve
certain problems.

It is safe to say that most children love electronic media, including TV,
CDs, DVDs, computer games and activities, and video games. For many
children with autism spectrum disorders, computer and video games hold
a special appeal. Parents have often commented that their children would
sit in front of an electronic screen for the better part of the day without
stopping to eat or sleep if they were allowed to. Certainly, this level and
intensity of electronic engagement isn't recommended, but there are

some advantages and opportunities for incorporating technology into skill-building, problem-solving, and therapeutic interventions, including Replays.

What is so appealing for all children – but especially for children with autism – is that computer and video games:

- are visually stimulating
- are fast-moving
- include music and interesting sound effects
- have explicit goals
- challenge players to experiment, think, and strategize
- provide immediate gratification
- include characters who are usually easy to understand: they are good, evil, smart, silly, angry, generous, etc.
- include characters with special and supernatural powers
- create entire new worlds with new rules
- give the child a sense of power
- offer a more appealing alternative to a child's reality.

Another advantage of the use of video games is the fact that many children, with and without disabilities, play them. So they may serve as an equalizer, uniting children with cognitive, perceptual, and neurological differences with their typically developing peers. One typical ten-year-old formed a friendship with a neighbor with high-functioning autism "because he was the only one who can beat me in video games, so I never get bored."

Can gaming be therapeutic?

Several families have reported that their children are more open to approaching a problem and attempting to solve it if the language or images used are recognizable and familiar – like those of their favorite video characters. One mother toilet-trained her twins, both with a diagnosis of PDD–NOS, by setting up a reward system that included duplicating the prizes awarded to the winning characters in a favorite video game. A stay-at-home father couldn't get his extremely active and inattentive son to help clean up until he played the music (which he downloaded to his own computer) from an action-packed game that included competing characters driving fast around corners, skiing, and swimming. The father of a four-year-old with autism reported that his son didn't catch on to cause and effect or turn-taking "in real life" until he mastered those concepts in a computer game.

A reward versus a means to an end

Too often gaming, like favorite television programs, is used only as a reward for compliance and appropriate behavior (or taken away for inappropriate behavior), rather than as a means for problem solving, improving understanding of self and others, and teaching or modeling social skills. Combining interventions such as Replays with gaming is not an approach that will work for every child or family, but it can improve certain behaviors and interactions, and help both adults and typically developing children connect with those with autism, Asperger's syndrome and related challenges. Electronic games can also serve as a means by which children with autism and related disorders can connect with each other.

Candace had always attended her neighborhood school with local, mostly typically developing, children. While they always accepted and never teased her, neither did they invite her to play or join in activities at school or on weekends. Every day she spent lunch and recess alone, swinging on the swings or walking around the periphery of the schoolyard. Now almost 12, some of her teachers began to notice changes that suggested that Candace was feeling depressed and left out, something her parents had always insisted was true.

Previously, many teachers and even the school guidance counselors had assured her parents that "Her classmates ask her to play, but she really prefers to be alone." Candace's parents didn't accept that explanation. They noticed that she often watched her peers from her living-room window, and would run up to them when she and her family encountered them at the mall. Rather than greeting her friends with a "Hi. What's up?" she would jump up and down repeatedly and screech, which was her way, her mother explained, of connecting and letting them know she was happy and excited to see them.

Although she had not acquired the social skills needed to interact appropriately with peers much of the time, Candace was extremely skilled at creating and manipulating virtual people in one of her favorite video games. Her favorite game was "Hollywood High" in which characters can be created and given dialogue, although several different games have similar useful properties for this purpose. She was brilliant at figuring out the tools they needed to acquire in order to get to the next level, save another virtual character or complete a mission. She understood their motivations, and how and when they might take the wrong path or make an irreversible mistake. Why, then, was it so difficult to interact with real people?

Candace's mother, somewhat of a "techie," herself, decided to use Candace's strengths to help her better understand the real world. She started with what might seem like a simple task for a typical pre-teen: meeting a friend at the mall and inviting her to lunch at a fast-food restaurant. She "customized" a character in a computer game and wrote a social script for the character:

Girl A (Candace): Hi. What's up?

Girl B: Nothing much. What's up with you?

Girl A: I want to go out for a hamburger. Can you join me?

Girl B: Sure. I'd love to go with you.

Girl A: That would be awesome!

Candace watched and manipulated the scenario many, many times, changing the girls' hairstyles, clothes, and jewelry. Her mother helped alter the dialogue so they could sample different scenarios and come up with different responses:

Girl A: Hi. I am in a hurry now. Would you like to meet for lunch another time?

Girl B: Yes. Thanks.

And another variation:

> Girl B: I can't go out with you today. I'm busy.

> Girl A: Oh. I'm sad. Maybe tomorrow.

Candace became upset initially when things didn't go smoothly the first time for her virtual self, but eventually she was able to tolerate her character's disappointment.

Other electronic solutions

Often children with communication and social difficulties truly want to interact with their peers but have never learned "the rules of engagement." Despite performing admirably in the school-based, once-a-week social skills group, it is difficult to remember all the steps needed for a successful conversation or play interaction during recess or after school at the park. Using a Dictaphone or small tape-recorder to record actual scripts can help. They can also serve as suggestions or cues for a child who doesn't know what to say next or has trouble retrieving the right words in the moment. In the following situation, Kevin, an elementary school student with mild autism and some social challenges, wanted desperately to play with Kim, a girl he had admired from afar, alone – in other words, without his aide constantly cueing him. The aide facilitated several short interactions first and then recorded one with Kim's cooperation. The idea was that Kevin could listen to it over and over before trying it on his own:

> Kim: Hi Kevin. (She sees Kevin with a colorful bottle of bubble liquid and a wand.) Let's play bubbles.

> Kevin: I like bubbles. (He hands her the bottle and mimes blowing bubbles, which she does several times.)

> Kim: Wow! That's a big one! Now you go. (She hands him the bottle and he tries, having more difficulty than she did and fumbling with the bubbles.) Come on. Hurry up. I want another turn.

> Kevin: I need help. Help. Help.

Kim: OK... Watch me. (She takes another turn, filling the air with bubbles, to his delight.)

Kevin: I want to do it. (He tries again, spilling some but eventually blowing a few small bubbles.)

Kim: Yay! You did it! Try again! (She pops the bubbles and claps.)

This simple, turn-taking play interaction lasted for most of the recess period, about ten minutes. And while the recorded Replay was orchestrated, supported, and directed by the aide, Kevin's playing it repeatedly helped him eventually engage in a social interaction as well as learning some important skills: waiting, taking turns, asking for help, and trying again and again until he succeeded. Not only did he succeed in blowing bubbles; he also got a positive reaction and the much-needed acceptance of his classmate.

Kevin's aide has used a tape-recorder in similar situations with consistent success. Kevin has learned to raise his hand to answer questions in class, have a short conversation at snack time, and ask to join a game of tetherball after school.

Other technical applications for Replays

- Multi-player video games are ideal for "practicing" many of the Replays discussed throughout the book (e.g. needing to win or lose, perfectionism). The adult or two peers can take turns purposefully driving off the course or crashing their characters etc., to practice the issue that is so challenging in real life. Caricatures of feared objects and situations (e.g. clowns; bugs; birthday parties; fire alarms) can be created in many different kinds of games, with characters having extreme reactions on screen.

- Use of video can be incorporated into Replays in many different ways. Adults or older peers or siblings can video the child just beginning to become interested in Replays. Children often love watching the Replays played back on video, experiencing them all over again with delight. This can help reinforce the impact and further teach the symbolic aspect.

- Older children can enjoy videotaping the dramatic role-play acting scenes of their Replays.

- Video can also be incorporated as part of the dramatic play. For example, the adult can use a commercial video or make a video clip of things that are scary to the child, and then play them without volume on a tiny screen while the adult pretends to cover his or her eyes, if this is funny to the child, again increasingly approximating reality.

13

Frequently Asked Questions

In this section, we will address questions that people often ask when we are introducing Replays, or after people have been using them. Most of the information is contained in more detail in the rest of the book. This section is intended to be a quick resource.

Do Replays ever increase unwanted behavior?

Doing Replays may initially cause an increase in the undesired behavior, just as introducing a new behavioral plan can cause the child to "push the limits." But this usually doesn't happen. We think this is because the replayed behaviors and the scenario itself are already "near and dear" to the child – that is, Replays incorporate behaviors that the child engages in frequently. For example, if a child does well with haircuts, one wouldn't introduce Replays around a child having a haircut tantrum. Replays provide a new – and for most children – an interesting and more fun way to participate in and learn alternatives to an uncomfortable or disruptive behavior.

When do you do Replays?

It is usually most effective to do Replays after the upsetting event or undesirable behavior has occurred, when the child is calm and has moved on. For example, for a child who gets upset around haircuts, the day after a haircut start doing Replays, then the week before the next one do Replays in many variations (with parents, dolls, siblings) many times.

Sometimes, Replays can be done during a mildly upsetting event or when the child has just begun to be mischievous. This is most likely to be effective in situations where the child has almost mastered control. For example, for a child who dislikes diaper changes, Replays can be done between them. However, starting a Replay with a tantruming doll, just as the child starts to object, can be both distracting and prevent the real tantrum from escalating. For a child trying to leave a playroom or struggle out of a car seat, immediately have a "buddy character" join the child in this (have Elmo or Spider-Man® HATE his car seat and struggle to get out). This "Instant Replay" is easier to do with two adults but can – and we speak from experience – be done with one! Creating a story and other re-enactments can be done later.

Are there children for whom Replays are especially likely to be effective?

Children with anxiety, Asperger's, PDD–NOS, autism, obsessive compulsive disorder (OCD), sensory integration disorder, behavioral problems secondary to ADHD, and language delays are all excellent candidates for Replays. Typically developing children also find Replays enjoyable and benefit from their use for typical behavior problems (e.g. not wanting to take medicine; go to bed; turn off the TV, etc.) (see, for example, Chapter 10 on using Replays with siblings, and Chapter 11 on using Replays in the classroom).

Children who are young enough to enjoy play with dolls and action figures are also likely to benefit; however there are tricks to get older children involved (e.g. using age-appropriate movie-tie-in action figures and superheroes, and more disguised themes. Spider-Man® can be afraid of a huge jump between buildings for an eight-year-old afraid of going swimming; Barbie® can be afraid to go to a party for a 12-year-old socially anxious girl). See Chapter 5 on using Replays with older and more verbal children. Most children still enjoy pretend play well beyond the preschool years as long as they are able to feel it isn't "babyish." Consider, for example, the large number of adults who play role-playing computer games, and enjoy animated movies and community acting. There is no "ceiling" of development on the use of pretend as long as it is done through a medium that is of great appeal to the child.

Can Replays be used in conjunction with a behavior plan to treat the same behavior?

Yes. Replays combined with positive behavioral supports are often very effective. The child afraid of haircuts can do lots of Replays in between haircuts AND be promised stickers afterwards. The child who won't wear his or her glasses can be rewarded for wearing them initially for a few minutes at a time and also do a lot of Replays around this. The behavioral supports help highlight for the child what you want them to do and how proud you are of their accomplishments. Also the Replays make it easier for them to actually do what you want and to develop coping strategies by mastering their emotional challenges around the event. In addition, simple consequences such as "time out" for aggression combined with a reward system can readily complement Replays.

Can Replays be combined with an Applied Behavioral Analysis (ABA) "Discrete Trials" teaching approach?

Yes. Replays can be done at the table as a "break" within running programs. This format can be especially useful for children with short attention spans, who have learned to attend well in this table-top teaching format. Replays can be done at other times for children in ABA programs, but not within the teaching time. Replays can also be used to help children with aspects of dicrete trial teaching that they may not initially like. For example, try getting a resistant child into a chair by having Winnie the Pooh not want to sit in the chair, then climb in and have fun. Or make Elmo reluctantly put a block in a bucket, modeling for the child who knows how to do this but won't.

Can Replays be combined with a DIR (Developmental, Individual-difference, Relationship-based)/Floor Time approach?

Replays are very consistent with the principles of DIR Floor Time, as the focus is on accessing and advancing the child's emotional developmental system through meaningful affective interactive symbolic play. Replays, however, are more structured and adult-directed than most activities within a DIR/Floor Time approach. However, while the adult in Replays is not following the child's lead within the play, the theme of the play is developed according to the child's interests.

Can Replays be combined with an Relationship Development Intervention (RDI® Program) approach?

Replays is an additional tool that can readily be used with most children who are also learning through use of RDI® activities. It works because the emotional engagement between the adult and child is highlighted, expanded in content, and extended in time. But unlike most RDI® activities, which are developed to expand the child's social pragmatic development, the focus of Replays is on teaching emotional coping through use of symbolic play, related to specific troubling situations.

Is Replays consistent with practice in the SCERTS® model?

Yes. Replays is remarkably consistent with priority goals and strategies in the SCERTS® model framework (Prizant *et al.* 2006), as SCERTS® is designed to incorporate a range of effective therapeutic and educational strategies. First and foremost, the Emotional Regulation (ER) domain directly addresses negative emotional memories that may be dysregulating factors for a child. Replays targets reduction of such negative emotional memories that may result in refusal, avoidance or protest behaviors through playful practice and desensitization. Second, the SC domain of SCERTS addresses the development and use of symbolic play skills as a priority goal area, quite consistent with the play-based approach used in Replays. Finally, the TS of the SCERTS®

model utilizes clearly defined Interpersonal Supports across partners to foster a child's social and emotional development, and Replays is largely predicated on specific interpersonal support strategies, which can be applied across a variety of partners and contexts.

Can Replays be used with children who don't have pretend play skills?

Often children who are not spontaneously or independently doing pretend play will "get" Replays as the themes being played are so familiar and intensely experienced by the child (see Chapter 4 on Replays for younger or less verbal children).

Are there any behaviors that Replays shouldn't be used for?

Children engaging in particularly dangerous behaviors with an aware-ness of the danger aspect (e.g. fire setting; stealing money; severe aggression with an awareness of the severity; suicidal gestures) gener-ally have more complex issues than Replays would be recommended for. Children with such behaviors respond well to other interventions and therapy but not Replays, because the root causes are very different from the behaviors described in this book.

Are there any children Replays shouldn't be used for?

Some children with severe mood disorders including Bipolar Disorder can become "stuck on" the acting-out of the anger or frustration, and this can trigger an agitated episode. Children with mild regulatory issues, and some children with more significant mood issues, also including Bipolar Disorder, however, can be helped by Replays. For children for whom there is concern about triggering anger, we recom-mend starting Replays with issues that are not typical triggers for the child and gradually moving to more upsetting issues, beginning by using props and characters more abstractly related to the child (e.g.

dinosaurs rather than people figures), and monitoring the child's response. Working closely with a psychotherapist initially to explore what sort of play is helpful is strongly recommended for children with more significant mood disorders.

Some children with thought disorders find it confusing to change roles or have characters act like them. However, Replays can be helpful for some children with thought disorders especially during times when they are more "connected" and oriented. During these times, playing through specific, frequently occurring situations that cause confusion can be very helpful. For example, we worked with a child who had a thought disorder but often had quite lucid times, and had heightened sound sensitivity. When she was in a more confused state, she misinterpreted sounds but, when she was more lucid, she simply had an anxious strong startle response. We used Replays to work on the sound sensitivity just as described in Chapter 8, and it was quite effective across several situations even during less lucid times. Replays will not fix the thought disorder but can be tools for treating associated challenges.

Does Replays work right away or does it take a long time? How many times should you do it?

Sometimes Replays works right away. This is most likely to be true for Replays around frequently occurring sensory issues that the child has physiologically but not emotionally outgrown (e.g. a four-year-old who always has a meltdown around putting his shoes on even though they no longer feel aversive). Similarly, Replays can work very quickly for phobias around issues that once were scary to the child but are no longer actually scary, although the anticipation continues to lead to anxiety and associated fear (e.g. child with a longstanding fear of bugs stemming from a long ago bug bite or being startled long ago; haircut fear). When Replays works quickly, even within a single play session, it is quite amazing to see and gratifying for all involved!

Sometimes the impact of Replays is more gradual, and then when it is done over and over, tinkered with to hold the child's interest, over time (e.g. weeks), it works. This gradual change is more typical for situations that are truly aversive for children (e.g. not being first for a child with obsessive issues) in the moment. Playing the Replays many times, in between actual experiences, combining this with other approaches (behavioral rewards; Social Stories™) leads to more gradual change. For situations that are aversive to the child, Replays can diminish the build up of fear and anxiety but may not help the actual situation (e.g. a child who is extremely sensitive to sounds may still cry when everyone claps at a party, or cover his ears at the movies, but may, through Replays, be able to attend the party or movie without spending the whole time anticipating the dreaded sounds.

Sometimes when Replays aren't working, it is important to revisit the problem event to make sure one is Replaying the actual challenging aspect of the situation. We did Replays around going on the school bus for one child who had a tantrum each morning getting on the bus, but then was fine for the rest of the day. It turned out, as he became more verbal, he was able to tell us he was upset about issues at the start of the school day, which he knew followed shortly after getting on the bus, and not the bus trip itself. Hence, adjusting the play as well as making small changes to his school day resolved the problem.

Is it appropriate for therapists (physical therapists, occupational therapists, and speech therapists) to incorporate Replays?

Yes. Occupational therapists can be especially effective using Replays around issues for children involving heightened sensory sensitivities. Speech therapists can incorporate all kinds of Replays, because this activity not only works on the child's emotions and behavior but also enhances symbolic play and communication skills. Physical therapy can be ideal for including Replays especially for active children (see Chapter 6). These therapists can provide useful input to families, teachers, and assistants regarding successful use of Replays and, likewise, families, teachers, and assistants can describe specific challenging situations that lend themselves to solutions through Replays.

Can Replays be done by psychologists and social workers?

Yes. Replays is a form of play therapy adapted for children who don't naturally use symbolic play to work through emotionally challenging issues. Play is the natural medium for psychologists and social workers with young typically developing children. Learning and using Replays can readily be incorporated into these practices. When parents or other therapists are first learning Replays, if they are not having success, it can be helpful to consult a child psychologist or social worker familiar with related play therapy techniques and this population.

Can parents do Replays just from reading this book or even certain chapters?

Yes. Many parents have been to a lecture on Replays, *and* have gone home and used it successfully the same night! Some behaviors and some children are more complicated, so more "tinkering" is needed, and it can be helpful to work with a child's other teachers or therapists to work out how to make it successful. Play therapists, speech therapists, and occupational therapists are often familiar with related techniques and are likely to be helpful.

Some adults are more naturally able to do the "play acting" aspect of Replays while for others it takes practice. The important thing to remember is not to worry about feeling like you are making a fool of yourself, and also that if you "mess up" you can just try again. As a general rule of thumb, the more playful you are in a way the child can appreciate, the more the child will be amused and fascinated, the less anxious they will be, and the more effective the Replays will be. If you are having trouble, you might be able to find someone who can get the child started (e.g. a friend, older sibling or a person from the child's school). Once the child knows the game, it is easier to expand and introduce new Replays.

Reference

Prizant, B.M., Wetherby, A.M., Rubin, E., Laurent, A.C. and Rydell, P.J. (2006) *The SCERTS Model: Volume I Assessment; Volume II Program Planning and Intervention.* Baltimore, MD: Brookes Publishing.

Subject Index

Author Index